FALSIFIED

THE DANGER OF FALSE CONVERSION

Vincent and Lori Williams

Copyright © 2012 Vincent and Lori Williams

All rights reserved. No part of this book may be used or reproduced by any means, graphic, electronic, or mechanical, including photocopying, recording, taping or by any information storage retrieval system without the written permission of the publisher except in the case of brief quotations embodied in critical articles and reviews.

Unless noted otherwise: Scripture quotations taken from the New American Standard Bible®, Copyright © 1960, 1962, 1963, 1968, 1971, 1972, 1973, 1975, 1977, 1995 by The Lockman Foundation. Used by permission." (www.Lockman.org)

WestBow Press books may be ordered through booksellers or by contacting:

WestBow Press
A Division of Thomas Nelson
1663 Liberty Drive
Bloomington, IN 47403
www.westbowpress.com
1-(866) 928-1240

Because of the dynamic nature of the Internet, any web addresses or links contained in this book may have changed since publication and may no longer be valid. The views expressed in this work are solely those of the author and do not necessarily reflect the views of the publisher, and the publisher hereby disclaims any responsibility for them.

Any people depicted in stock imagery provided by Thinkstock are models, and such images are being used for illustrative purposes only.

Certain stock imagery © Thinkstock.

ISBN: 978-1-4497-3535-7 (sc)
ISBN: 978-1-4497-3536-4 (hc)
ISBN: 978-1-4497-3534-0 (e)

Library of Congress Control Number: 2011963163

Printed in the United States of America

WestBow Press rev. date: 02/09/2012

Contents

Foreword By Justin Peters ix

Introduction: A Brief look at False Conversion xv

Chapter 1-Our Testimonies of His Story in Us 1

Chapter 2-The Seeker Driven/Seeker Sensitive Movement 6

Chapter 3-The Biblical Approach to Church 24

Chapter 4-An Eye Opening Experience on Hollywood Blvd .. 28

Chapter 5-Evangelism: The Great Commission & Commandment 31

Chapter 6-Word of Faith & The Prosperity Gospel 36

Chapter 7-Hypocrisy Vs. Living the Word 42

Chapter 8-Sin, Judgment, and Hell 46

Chapter 9-The Gospel (or Good News) of Jesus Christ 51

Chapter 10-A Call to Men 56

Chapter 11-A Call to Women 66

Epilogue 77

Appendix 85

Tips on Tracting 97

Recommended Resources Page 99

Links Showing Examples of Seeker Sensitive Churches 101

Links to Great Preachers Boldly Preaching the Word 107

Bibliography 109

Dedication:

*We would like to dedicate this book to the following,
Our Lord and Savior Jesus Christ for granting us eternal salvation and opening our eyes to truth. Without Him, this book would not even be possible, may all the glory go to Him for any outcome of this venture.*

Dr.John MacArthur-For preaching solid biblical truth and never backing down. For showing us what it means to be disciples of the Word through your preaching and ministry. May Grace Community Church continue to be blessed. The day we were able to visit was truly one of the best days of our lives. What a God Honoring Church!

Justin and Kathy Peters-thank you for being the needle in the haystack. Your friendship has been a breath of fresh air and we thank you for allowing us to be your roadies. You mean more to us than words can ever express.

Dustin Aldridge-Thank you for bringing truth to us over and over, patiently being a solid Christian friend who's gone through a lot with us.

Our Families-Terrill, Cathy, Ron, Suzy, Lisa, Mike, Clint and Elizabeth: Thank you for being a family that loves us always and for what you've taught us in life. We are grateful to have two sets of parents still married after many years and have taught us many lessons about marriage. You mean so much to us and we love you dearly.

And thank you to the following people for the roles and things they have done in our lives: Phil Johnson for his advice, endorsement, and humility to share his story and encourage us in this book. Brannon Howse for standing strong even when it means standing alone. Justin Peters, thank you for taking the time to write the foreword amidst your busy schedule and letting us ride in your big white Sprinter box at 3:00am while we sleep and you drive. And to Kathy for putting up with two severe wretches—we Chief, you Indian.

To both of you—"This one's for papaw"

Art Azurdia, Steve Lawson, Emilio Ramos, Paul Washer, Mark Hitchcock and RW Glenn for being some of our favorite pastors. Ray Comfort for teaching us the biblical way to evangelize.

And lastly . . . to Joel Osteen . . . thank you for, I don't know, um I don't know, well I don't know . . . .

Foreword
By Justin Peters

One of the world's most popular "evangelical" preachers enthusiastically opined "I see faith in America at an all-time high."¹ Recent decades have seen a rise in the number of megachurches which offer entertaining services featuring contemporary music and are led by oratorically talented preachers possessing winsome personalities.² Books which deal with spirituality and religion are flying off the shelves and often sit atop the New York Times bestsellers list for months at a time. The United States of America is widely considered to be a Christian nation. But it's not true – none of it. It's a façade. Behind the services offering state-of-the-art media technology, contemporary and upbeat music combined with practical, "relevant" sermons, true biblical Christianity is dying.

---

1. Cheryl Wetzstein, "Osteen: Americans' faith at 'all-time high,'" *The Washington Times*, October 24, 2011. In this article Joel Osteen, pastor of Lakewood Church in Houston, TX, is also quoted as affirming that Mormons are Christians; this despite the fact that Mormonism denies many of the fundamental doctrines of historical Christianity.
2. Source: http://www.forbes.com/2009/06/26/americas-biggest-megachurches-business-megachurches.html According to this article

According to numerous recent studies, a shockingly high percentage of children raised in evangelical churches are leaving the church upon leaving the home. Most of the children and youth in church today will not be in the pews tomorrow. According to Barna, 61% of today's young adults who regularly attended church as children are now "spiritually disengaged."[3] Many of these are professing believers who have been baptized. Something is terribly wrong and there is no reason to expect this disturbing trend to change. It is only getting worse.

Some fifty or so years ago a trend began to emerge among many evangelical pulpits. Preachers slowly but surely began to abandon the preaching of God's holiness and wrath as the primary means to lead sinners to repentance and faith in Christ. The preaching of wrath and coming judgment fell out of favor because it was seen as too harsh and unfriendly. Preachers became increasingly reticent to offend the sensibilities of their congregants. They wanted their churches and denominations to grow and prosper and telling people that they were sinners who had offended an angry God and in peril of eternal punishment was not seen as conducive to those goals. So, many pulpits began to offer a kinder, gentler gospel: Come to Jesus because He will give you a better life; He will fill the "God-shaped" hole in your heart; Know Jesus, know peace – no Jesus, no peace; God will give you prosperity and healing; God will give you a purpose driven life; God loves you and has a wonderful plan for your life.

Of course, this was done to varying degrees by varying churches and denominations. Some softened more than others to be sure. However, over the years and decades, the trend continued. Like the proverbial frog in the pot of water slowly heating up to the boiling point, most people did not notice and few raised objections. Generations have now been raised under soft preaching. Generations of parents in Christian homes have outsourced their responsibility to teach their children the Bible to Sunday School teachers and youth ministers. Now, however, the

---

[3] Source: The Barna Group, LTD 2006.

water is boiling. Most professing Christians today are stunningly ignorant of basic Christian doctrine and are biblically illiterate. Most do not know what they really believe and have even less idea of why they believe it. Most are incapable of giving a reason for the hope that, they say, is within them (1 Peter 3:15). Some faithful preachers and laymen have been sounding the alarm but the point of no return may well have already been reached. The softening of the Gospel has led inexorably to theological and doctrinal compromise. The seeds which have been sown in the last half-century are now reaping a harvest of biblically ignorant, theologically confused, uncommitted and unconcerned masses with a post-modern worldview. Many of these "spiritually disengaged" still identify as being Christian but only in the loosest sense of the term. Their values, beliefs and lifestyles bear little resemblance to the Christianity recorded in Scripture. The disciples and apostles of the New Testament knew what they believed, were devoted to the reading and study of Scripture, and preached the Gospel boldly in the face of severe persecution. Their convictions cost them their lives. Today's Christianity bears little resemblance to that which marked the early church.

Though exceptions certainly do (thankfully) exist, most preachers today have softened the message of the Gospel. They have lowered the bar. Being a "Christian" today is far easier and requires far less sacrifice than it ever has before. Today, most people think they are Christians because they were raised in church, or because they prayed the "sinner's prayer" and were baptized at some point in their lives - most often childhood. As the years pass, however, there is little if any evidence of true conversion. There is little if any conviction of sin, love for God and the study of His Word, love for the church, self-denial – in short, there is no transformation. If there is no transformation, there is no true conversion. Today's churches are filled with people claiming to be Christian, many of whom truly believing that they are, but in reality are false converts.

False conversion is an epidemic in the church today. Millions have been given a gospel that is lite on sin, lite on repentance and heavy on life enhancement. Millions have responded. Millions are false converts. This watered-down, easy to believe "gospel" is really no Gospel at all. It is a different gospel with a different message which promotes a different Jesus. This is why Christianity looks so profoundly different today than what it has looked like historically. Truth be known, today's Christianity (especially the American version)[4] is, in some ways, not unlike Hinduism. Hindus believe in millions of gods and are often perfectly happy to add Jesus to their long list of deities but do not believe Him to be the sovereign Creator and Redeemer. Many Christians today are perfectly happy to add Jesus to their lives as long as He fits in somewhere and does not cause any major disruptions or demands any real sacrifice.

The problem of false conversion is the theological elephant sitting in the living room of evangelical Christianity. Many are aware of the problem but few have the courage to address it in a meaningful way. It is an immense problem that is getting worse. Weak preaching produces false converts who seek out more doctrinally weak churches (if they seek out churches at all) which must continue to soften the Gospel to attract more false converts. It is a vicious cycle which shows no signs of being broken. That is the bad news. The good news, though, is that some *are* sounding the alarm. Some *do* care. There is and always will be a remnant of faithful preachers who rightly divide the Word of Truth (2 Tim. 2:15) for God's faithful remnant who desire it and will not settle for anything less. The power to right the ship *is* available – it always has been. The power of God *is* the *Gospel*. As bleak as the plight of today's church may seem, there

---

[4] I have been to many countries where Christianity is not the social norm and is often persecuted. Though the percentage of people claiming to be Christian is far lower in these nations, the Christians one does find tend to be far more dedicated and have a far better understanding of what biblical Christianity really is. Christians who experience persecution take their faith seriously because it comes at a cost.

are rays of hope. There seems to be underfoot a move of God to awaken His people from their spiritual slumber. There seems to be a growing number of young people who are being awakened to the dangers of false conversion and who take doctrine seriously. Their lives are being transformed. Vince and Lori Williams are two such examples. Both of them were false converts led into a false sense of security by seeker-sensitive churches preaching a watered-down gospel. God, in His sovereign grace, opened their spiritual eyes, saved them, and gave them new hearts which yearn to know Him by knowing His Word. They have a burden to warn others to flee from the dangers of false conversion to which they fell victim. They know its deception and harm by first-hand experience. They know its deception and harm by first-hand experience. My wife, Kathy, and I are privileged to be their sister and brother in Christ and honored to count them as dear friends. *Falsified* is their story.

Introduction

A Brief look at False Conversion

> *"Not everyone who says to Me, 'Lord, Lord, will enter the kingdom of heaven, but he who does the will of My Father who is in heaven will enter."* Matthew 7:21

False Conversion? This is not a term that you would hear in the contemporary church in the 21st century, however it is exactly what is going on in most "evangelical" churches today. It is an issue that is polluting the very heart of the American church and we fell victim to it. This book is meant and designed to help equip people to understand what false conversion looks like, the seeker driven movement that helps promote it, and the correct and proper way to combat it, which is, the Gospel.

First we need to define false conversion. The idea that a person is saved simply because they have been led into the "sinner's prayer", baptized or even affirmed by someone, does not mean that they are in fact saved. There are many common phrases people use to describe their conversion, "I've accepted Jesus into my heart", "I walked the aisle", "I grew up in church", and the all famous classic . . . . "I'm a good person, so I know that I'm going to heaven" are just a few examples.

Not one of these terms or ideas can be found anywhere in Scripture, which we will go into later in the book, but this gives you a good idea of how the majority of "Christians" talk and the lingo that is used to define their spirituality. This is where the danger of false conversion comes into play. Many church-going people are duped into this belief that they are saved, when in essence so many have been falsely confirmed into this thought. That is exactly what happened to us.

Chapter 1

Our Testimonies of His Story in Us

We were married in June of 2008. We both thought we were soundly saved and thus ready to embark on the adventure of being married. It was evident by our actions early into marriage that we clearly began to see that things were not as they seemed -in either of us. Something was clearly wrong and missing at the heart of who we were. There was one fact that was apparent and that was that we were not saved. We were walking around claiming the name of Jesus, but completely disregarding His word and His commandments. We individually came to a true saving faith in the early winter of 2009. We would like to share our testimonies first so that you as the reader can see why we have a passion about this topic and feel the need to expose a lot of what you will read in some of the other chapters. Having been falsely confirmed for so long is something we do not want to happen to others. Therefore parts of this book may seem judgmental and hard to read. It is the urgency in needing to bring the truth to light is where the passion and the strong tone will come from.

Vince's Testimony of false to true conversion:

When I was 5 yrs old, I was at a "revival" meeting at the church my family was attending. The evangelist there gave an invitation after his message and I vividly remember getting up from my seat, going down with one of my parents to the altar and saying a prayer. I have no recollection of what I said or what his message was about, but what I found out about 23 yrs later is that I was a victim of false conversion.

From the time I was five I would grow up in a Christian home and would continue to go to church regularly because it was the "right Christian" thing to do. However, obviously growing up in a Christian home is no guarantee of salvation, but can be a recipe for self-righteousness. I simply continued trying to live a good moral life the best I could, but I still loved my sin, and lived for myself and not for the Lord. In John 14:15 Jesus says "If you love Me, you will keep my commandments" and again in verse 23 of the same chapter, He says "if anyone loves me, he will keep My word," verse 24, "He who does not love Me does not keep My words . . . .". I was like the Pharisees that Jesus spoke to in John 8, about their hypocrisy, when he told them "You are of your father, the devil, and you want to do the desires of your father."

In the summer of 2006, after years of sinful living and rebelling against God I came to the end of myself and cried out to God to show me the way. I told Him I wanted my life to be different, that I had really messed up, that I could not do it on my own, and I wanted Him to take control. However, that point in time was not yet His pre-ordained time for my salvation. There was a 180 change in my life, but it was a somewhat moral change. I still wanted to do some of the things that I was previously into and the Lord was not first in my life. My mind was changed to some degree but my heart was not. I had not yet turned from sin because in 2 Corinthians 5 Paul tells us "Therefore if anyone is in Christ, he is a new creature; the old things passed away; behold, new things have come." For me in that time old things had not yet passed away. It was not until three years later, at the beginning of 2009, by His sovereignty that He saved me by revealing to me through His Holy Spirit and the Scriptures that I was a wretched sinner deserving of eternal torment in hell. This is warned about in many places in Scripture. I needed a Savior, Jesus Christ, whose perfect life could be credited to my account only through repentance and faith in Him. In John 3 Jesus says, "Unless one is born again he cannot see the kingdom of God." Again, as John 3 also talks about, I was never born of the Spirit. Finally, I repented, and I put my complete trust in Him, and His work on the cross, to save me. From then on there was a 180 change in my heart and my life. Old things had passed away and He gave me a new heart with new desires. He then further took me back to the Law of God in the Ten Commandments and how even those commandments are magnified in the Sermon on the Mount (for one example). Through that process He revealed even more to me the depths of my sin, which led me to more confession. All this has led me to an even deeper walk with Him and further growth in holiness by the power of the Holy Spirit in me. I praise and thank the Lord, and give Him ALL credit for my salvation.

Lori's Testimony:

I grew up in a "Christian home" and was brought up in church. I made the decision to "accept Christ into my heart" at the age 8 out of respect to my parents. The decision was to please them but I did not fully understand the gospel at that time. However, I know now that I was not truly saved at that time. I did not understand the law of God and how much of a sinner that I was in rebellion to my Lord. Many people in the church, including the pastor that baptized me, all just asked if I had asked Jesus to come live inside in me but never once talked to me about my sin. I remember my Sunday school teacher taking me in the room after I walked the aisle and went through a picture book that basically glamorized the Gospel. No one or any of the material shown was making sure that this 8-year-old girl fully understood the Gospel. It was all focused on what Jesus could do for me, not what I had done to Him. I always believed in Jesus, but it was all head knowledge and moral living. I failed to repent and understand the gospel in its entirety. It was in the time frame of early winter 2009 that I know that I truly came to know Christ in the way the gospel is explained in the Bible. Vince and I had been doing some lifestyle changes in the way of the church we attended, the things we watched, read, and listened to. It was through that time we heard a message from Paul Washer that he is best known for, the shocking sermon he gave to the youth at a church. We had also started watching and listening to the Way of the Master (1) and I heard Ray Comfort talk about examining yourself before the 10 commandments. It was between those two events, that I fully grasped the Gospel. I understood that it doesn't matter how much moral living I do, it would never make God love me more, and it would never open the gates of heaven to me wider. I was a wretched sinner and I needed a Savior to save me from my sin. I have fully repented and continue to live in that manner walking with Christ and in accordance to what He says about sin. I do not do this out of moral living obedience, but because every time I sin, I offend God. I have been fully forgiven of my sins but I also understand daily faith and repentance now. The fruit started to show up in a way it never did from age 8 to 28. I have such a heart for the lost now that I never did before. I used to have a hard heart against people that didn't "do the right thing.' I now realize I was no better than they are. The only thing that sets me apart from those living in their sin is that they love their sin. I hate sin now, and my heart and desires have changed because He saved me. He saved me from hell, and from myself. He saved me from living a life in total selfishness, to one that only wants to do the will of the Lord now and follow His commandments. I no longer dive into sin and then try to rationalize it and tip the scales with my good deeds. There is a decreased pattern of sin in my life and a love for the lost. I too want them to come to the saving grace of Jesus through repentance and trusting in Him. It changes your entire view of everything. I am so thankful that He not only chose to save me, but He did so at a time that He was saving my husband as well. We have never been the same; our marriage has never been the same. All credit is due to the Holy Lord Jesus.

As you can clearly see we were held hostage by the idea that we were soundly saved when we clearly were not. We were confirmed by our friends, family, and clergy that since we had prayed the sinner's prayer, which by the way is no where in the Bible, that we were rightly converted and on our way to heaven. Please stop and examine yourself, if you too have been living a moral life, or balancing the scales with your good works against your bad deeds. This is not the mark of a Christian, this is the mark of a false convert.

Chapter 2

The Seeker Driven/Seeker Sensitive Movement

> *Enter through the narrow gate: for the gate is wide and the way is broad that leads to destruction, and there are many who enter through it. For the gate is small and the way is narrow that leads to life and there are few who find it. Matthew 7:13-14*

The term seeker-sensitive refers to putting more importance on the "needs" of un-believers than on the need to teach the Word of God to believers, thus equipping believers to obey God's Word.

Let us describe what this movement looks like to the average person walking into a Seeker Style Church. Flashy lights, high octane and concert feeling music, no pulpit-just a relevant looking table, or maybe just a chair that the "pastor" speaks to you from. Typically there is a coffee bar or beverage table in the lobby that quickly makes you think of a coffee house environment. Hip chairs, modern color combinations and decorations with an industrial loft style feel is typical of most interiors of a seeker church. Often at these churches you will be greeted at the door with a happy high energy feel that instantly gets you pumped to "do church the new way."

Falsified

As you enter the gathering place for their "experience" you will notice dimmed lights so you don't feel too uncomfortable and can't be easily seen that you are new. Generally it's a very open setting with lots of chairs and rows so you can sit in the back and not be noticed or accountable to anyone. It's designed all for *you*. It is all be geared around what will seem hip and relevant to the outside person who has the "I hate traditional church" mentality and therefore they want to bring about a no pressure, "this is your other home" type of feeling in the place.

Once the experience starts you are quickly engaged into a song that everyone knows. It has turned into the time of the show where these wanna-be-rock stars try out the latest secular song and perform their hearts out. After you get warmed up and whipped up with the first song you go into the song that nobody knows, a new song that is hip and you can substitute the word Jesus for your boyfriend or girlfriend's name and won't know the difference. Sometimes even an original song that the worship leader just wrote, just for *you*! After you have been tranced into that effect, they bring it back up with the song that you learned the week before and now can repeat it easily and sing the chorus at least 10 times.

From there your campus pastor will come out and give you the latest updates and information of the hot new groovy things they have planned for *you*. This is all designed to get the entire rock band, also known as the worship team, off stage and get the stage cleared off for your very own church CEO/Vision Caster/Mega church or Lead Pastor to come on the scene. If you are lucky, he might actually be there in person, otherwise you are probably attending one of the multi site campuses and he's being piped in via flat screen simulcast or other media. Then he gives his very applicable "for *you*" message full of scriptures taken out of context, hip anecdotes, and even visual aides. You might even catch it on a Saturday night or Sunday experience where they are doing some sort of series. We have yet to visit or attend one of these seeker churches that are not in the middle of a cool new series of topical feel good help advice. If you are really lucky, you might just visit on a day when they are doing the "At the Movies" series. Most all seeker churches have adapted to this series meant to "draw the seeker in" where they take a movie that is well known to the public and they try to pull out Christian principles from it.

After you get your pep talk for the week or animated adventure (as some may call it) from the hipster pastor, they will then do a mass invitation. This is the interesting part about seeker churches, they are not always preaching a false Gospel, and we want to be careful to point that out. Not all of them preach heresy, but a lot of them do. Most do in fact talk about Jesus Christ, however it is how they present this information is what has become troublesome. There is typically not a mention of sin and a need for repentance in the call for the invitation. You will most likely hear about needing to be forgiven, but no clear explanation as to why or what it means to turn from your sins, therefore it ends up being Gospel-less. This is where it gets really concerning when you visit these seeker churches. You are invited to raise your hand "high high up in the air, with every eye closed and every head bowed" so that you can come to "know Jesus." Let me ask you this . . . aren't we supposed to be proud of our Savior and what He did for us? Why would we be so ashamed we only want the pastor to see us raise that hand and then quickly slip it back down? Once you come to a true saving faith and you realize that you are no longer bound for an eternity of hell and condemnation, you should be boldly shouting from the roof that" My God saved me!", not sheepishly holding a hand up in a dark auditorium where you most likely did not hear any form of the Gospel.

Once that part of the experience has been accomplished and you have been "counted" as being converted today by the speaker, you then get an invitation to go to the back after the service ends to get your welcome or new believers kit. This will include all kinds of freebies promoting the church's fun activities and all that they can do for *you*! But before that, an offering will be taken up where a popcorn bucket of sorts quickly is passed around and once again the rock stars enter the stage to entertain you while you give freely of your money.

At some of these seeker churches, they are so big they can't make time for the Lord's Supper, so they just have the elements sitting on the sides of the church. So during this serenade by the band you can go do a quick ten second communion completely devoid of any self-examination. We actually visited a seeker church in November of 2011 and a very kind woman introduced herself and was standing by the elements. Lori asked her how a non-Christian would know not to go over and partake of the elements. She said that sometimes its mentioned from the pulpit but that it is always in the bulletin. She unfolded the bulletin to try and find it; she could not find it anywhere. We all stood there looking at one another and she said, "well I have never thought of that." She was very kind hearted and genuine but you could see the light bulb click that it was not mentioned anywhere of the warning that the Lord's Table is only for true believers. She was concerned of this fact once she pieced it all together. We were encouraged that she was going to bring this to the attention of the leaders. There are many in these seeker churches just as we were that are kind to the core but just lost in all the flashiness of this style of church.

All of this described here generally happens in a span of just over an hour. They herd them in and herd them out so the next round of unsuspecting false converts can go be entertained and have their ears tickled. This should not surprise us since it says in:

> *2 Timothy 4:3-4*
> *"For the time will come when they will not endure sound doctrine, but wanting to have their ears tickled, they will accumulate for themselves teachers in accordance to their own desires, and will turn away their ears from the truth and will turn aside to myths."*

In addition it also states:

> *2 Timothy 3:5*
> *"holding to a form of godliness, although they have denied its power, Avoid such men as these."*

Lets look at the roots of this movement now that we know what it looks like in the modern day.

Donald McGavran is one of, if not the father of this movement. This taken from Ken Silva, founder of Apprising Ministries, in an article entitled "Fuller Theological Seminary Birthed Church Growth Movement" (2), he states:

> "McGavran founded the Institute of Church Growth, which in 1965 united with the Fuller School of World Mission. From there the pragmatic precepts of the church growth movement have reached into virtually every mission field worldwide. C. Peter Wagner, professor of church growth at the Fuller School of World Mission, is Donald McGavran's best-known student. Wagner is the most prolific if not the most influential spokesman in the church growth movement today."

Silva goes on to say in the same article, "The movement studies *all* growing churches—even those with false doctrine at the core of their teaching. Sometimes Mormon assemblies, Roman Catholic churches, even Jehovah's Witness Kingdom Halls are held up to the specialist's scrutiny. The church growth expert looks for characteristics common to all growing churches and advocates whatever methods seem to work. Are we to believe that growth in non-Christian congregations is proof that God is at work? Why would we want to duplicate the methodology of religious groups that deny the gospel? Isn't it fair to question whether any growth resulting from such methods is illegitimate, engineered by fleshly means? After all, if a method works as well for a cult as it does for the people of God, there's no reason to assume positive results signify God's blessing. Utterly missing from most of the church growth literature is any critical analysis of the faulty doctrinal platform on which much contemporary church growth is built."

The most recent followers of this movement are pastors Bill Hybels of Willow Creek Community Church and Rick Warren of Saddleback Church, both of which have helped launched this seeker driven movement. Let's look briefly at Bill Hybels first.

According to the Chicago Tribune in an article entitled "Rev. Bill Hybels: The father of Willow Creek" (3), it states, "He had had a powerful conversion experience, but he felt lonely within it because he couldn't relate it to the life of the church, which was my case also," Bilezikian said. Determined to spark excitement among adults and live out that vision, Hybels and a team of idealistic 20-somethings opened a new church in October 1975, naming it after the space they rented--Palatine's Willow Creek Theatre. They were cowboys, breaking rules and working hard to make church fun. Live bands and concise, practical sermons quickly earned Willow Creek a reputation for promoting "Christianity Lite."

The article continues to say, "In the late 1980s the national media caught wind of Willow's success, playing up its outreach to spiritual seekers as a "consumer-driven" approach to attract more "customers.' Also, "But the attention brought still more members, prompting the church to develop a small-group ministry that exists to this day to help newcomers find friends in the enormous congregation."

Now let's look at Rick Warren and his purpose driven church/life concept. In 1995 Rick Warren's The Purpose Driven Church launched into the public market being the number one best selling book of all time. According to the book Deceived on Purpose by Warren Smith (4), he says "Purpose Driven Church flyers were arriving in my mail box and showing up on community bulletin boards. Local churches were flying banners proclaiming they were "Purpose-Driven.' It seemed that everywhere I turned there was Rick Warren and his Purpose Driven Church." Mike Oppenheimer (5) says that, "Warren's seeker friendly philosophy is -Any visible differences between the Church and the world must be reduced to a minimum, this will make the church acceptable to the un-churched comfortable coming to the church. Making the terms neutral or acceptable is his main method. Tone down the language. Biblical words such as sinner, hell, etc. are kept to a minimum, so ones comfort is not jeopardized. This becomes a point of fear that one will drive them away with biblical language and meanings instead of attract them. This underestimates the work of the Spirit in converting the sinner with the word of truth that is to convict them of SIN. In fact it is a lack of faith in what God has spoken."

> 1 Timothy 1:6-7
> *"For some men, straying from these things, have turned aside to fruitless discussion, wanting to be teachers of the Law, even though they do not understand either what they are saying or the matters about which they make confident assertions."*
>
> Ephesians 5:6-7
>
> *"Let no one deceive you with empty words, for because of these things the wrath of God comes upon the sons of disobedience. Therefore do not be partakers with them."*

Oppenheimer goes on to say, "They call their evangelistic service a "seeker-sensitive service." We are told that they only want to make the gospel more attractive to the public consumer so they will come inside. Incorporating contemporary-style "Seeker Services" to draw in the unchurched from the community replaces the traditional Sunday worship service. They do not believe the people will respond unless they have their personal needs met, so their pain, loneliness, hurts, and self-fulfillment are concentrated on. If we can make them comfortable and happy they will stay in the church. These new church services create a non-challenging, comfortable environment for the "seeker" (the unsaved visitor). The congregation will purposely dress down avoiding ties, suits and dresses so that the average person can feel comfortable being there. We want them to know we are no that different from them. The main focus of this church growth policy is entertainment. Find the interest of the person and use this as a means to present the gospel (which has missing elements) to what is relevant to them personally. This is accomplished by preaching only positive messages!"

Continued in his article, Oppenheimer states "This is the opposite of what Paul said would help to influence people to 'make their decision' to follow Christ. *1 Corinthians 2:4-5: 'And my speech and my preaching were not with persuasive words of human wisdom, but in demonstration of the Spirit and of power.'* The Apostles did not attempt to entice the lost in the first century church with the frills they use today (music atmosphere to make them think we are like them). Even if they were available they would not use them."

Others have picked up on this trend of it's gaining popularity of over fourteen years now and are speaking out. For example, Ken Silva from Apprising Ministries (6) quotes Dr. John MacArthur, pastor of Grace Community Church in Sun Valley California as saying, "If you think it's foolishness and fun n' games and song n' dance and sermonettes for Christianettes—if you think it's that kind of stuff—that's what you're going to do; but if you know, as Al [Mohler] was saying, that the power is the truth, that God has, as we've heard all week, has invested his power, as R.C. [Sproul] said, in his Word, then that's what you preach. I mean, it's that simple! It comes down to this loss of preaching. And I'll tell you, how do you know it's the new liberalism? Because you can't stop a seeker-friendly movement, because it's going to be redefined, it's going to be redefined, it's going to be redefined . . . It's relentlessly being redefined because the culture changes so fast in a media-driven society. It changes so fast!"

You may be wondering how we know so much about this style of church and this movement that has run rampant in the evangelical community and it is because we had a first hand experience for many years being a part of it. Starting from around the year 2000 to 2008, we both were a part of a mega church in our own backyard in Oklahoma, for far too long. Both of us attended the same mega church, LifeChurch.tv, but not meeting each other until 2007.

Here is Lori's background into Life Church:

I had been actively attending my home church where I was trying to get plugged into their singles department. I would attend week after week seeing the same people and feeling quite awkward at the environment but nonetheless trying to do my moral church duty and check that off the box for the week. I would walk in having grown up with some of these people and seeing them fairly regularly only to be asked, "are you a visitor?", even after my name badge had been stuck on. One week they were praying for missions and asked that people get into groups of four or five and pray for about fifteen minutes for missions. Seemed like a simple enough idea to me, I looked around for some girls to group up with and pulled my chair over to where four girls were sitting and asked if I could join their group. I quickly was told "um . . . we already have four . . . but um I guess you can" in a rather snide and selfish way. My thoughts were, "I don't think the Lord is going to mind one more person praying for missions", but remained quiet and just swung my chair over. It was after this Sunday school service I decided to find something more comfortable, a place where I could be accepted and where I could find other people who felt the same way. Notice it was all about me. My motivation to seek out a new church was for me-not for the Lord and to study His word, but to find friends, to build my social life, to "meet people."

This is what drew me to LifeChurch, it was so formulated to me, the person who had been outcaste by their traditional church. There was a program entitled Day 3 that was widely popular with the singles in the metro area of Oklahoma City that was held at one of the LifeChurch campuses.

So there I was, driving almost 25 minutes after work to go to a seeker style singles group during the week. Many of these people at Day 3 were attendees of LifeChurch, therefore that is where I ended up spending my Sunday mornings or Saturday nights. It was comfortable for a single person to go there, no pressure, low lighting, no Gospel, nothing to move me out of my comfort zone. I could get up, drive over there, wear my t-shirt and jeans, and slip in the back and listen to relevant music and feel good messages. I could then leave and head on about my business knowing that I had fulfilled my duty for my church involvement that week. Nothing was threatening, no one was asking me to pray in public or how my life was going, it was just a modern church at it's best.

Fast forward a couple of years to around 2007 where I felt I needed to start getting a little more plugged in after hearing about "LifeGroups" and "you too can meet others just like YOU!" So I joined a co-ed singles Lifegroup where I met other people around my same age, all with the same focus I had . . . . me. We would do a canned lesson that the church gave out in the form of a dvd or notes to the Lifegroup leader, who had absolutely no qualifications to be leading a bible study. The first thirty minutes were usually a time of catching up and chatting about all the latest gossip and trends. I have to admit the people were very nice and I now realize that they were no better off than I was, we were all lost, we all needed a Savior and yet no one was teaching us any of that. We just thought we were doing the church thing right and therefore eternally saved. Nothing could be further from the truth. I had been in the group for about three months when it was September of 2007, this is where Vince enters the picture. Two hopelessly lost sinners thinking they were eternally secure were about to collide and never be the same.

I remember being one of the first to arrive at the house of the leader and in walks this new guy to the group with his friend. To be honest, I was quickly drawn to Vince but didn't think much of it until later on. He was cordial and we all introduced ourselves and my other girlfriends quickly began to show up to the group and we all engaged in our normal routine of catching up from the week. I did not know anything about Vince's walk with the Lord, I just noticed he had a Bible and it had tabs on it and it seemed well used . . . I definitely wanted to marry a Christian, so this guy was climbing the ladder. We became friends through the Lifegroup and I had been in charge of planning activities for the group. It was around the time of Halloween and of course I was going to plan a Halloween outing for the group. I can't even believe that I was so lost, I look back now and wonder why the Lord didn't just strike me down at that moment for leading so many people astray unknowingly. Combining a pagan celebration of a holiday with a social Christian outing . . . unbelievable. However, the Lord was about to bring Vince and I together.

Before we go any further Vince will share his way into LifeChurch.:

Mine will be brief since my involvement in the seeker-driven movement with Lifechurch is not much different than Lori's. We both left our traditional churches for the same reasons, both started going to Lifechurch for the same reason – to make church better and more enjoyable – for ME. It was all about ME. My Bible at the time may have had markings and tabs, etc. but it was only for show. I remember not too long after God graciously saved me I actually lost that Bible. When I look back it was probably a good thing since a hypocrite was using that particular Bible. I was talking about the Lord, but not living or doing what His Word prescribes. Lifechurch and the seeker-driven movement, for me, was a way of rebellion against God and my family. Similar to Lori, it was a way to improve my social network of friends, and do my "Christian" duty for the week. Lifechurch had everything I liked. This included rock music for worship songs (many of which were secular) hip "cool t-shirt and jeans at church" people just like me, and relevant messages that made me feel a part of something. They made me feel good, and enabled me to justify my sinful lifestyle because I was just another person who wanted to be a follower of Christ and live the way I wanted to live. I wanted to follow Christ, but still wanted to do what I wanted to do, not what Christ calls His followers to do. I did not go to Lifechurch to deny myself – to die to myself - and take up my cross, nor was I EVER told I needed to do so.

We ended up dating shortly after Halloween and knew we wanted to get married very soon. We even began getting more and more involved in LifeChurch, even teaching the fourth and fifth grade kids. That department was a disaster at how seeker driven the kid area had been marketed. They had more video games and interactive gear in one room than we knew what to do with. It was exercises and prizes and contests galore. No one needed their Bibles, even though we brought them every week.

We thought we were helping the kids by being a support for them to talk to, when all we did was be a glorified camp counselor for them. We went onto lead our very own Lifegroup for Singles and co-taught the group for over a year.

First off, we had no business being a teacher because we weren't saved. Secondly, we were not teaching biblical principles to our members, nor were we qualified to do so according to 2 Timothy 2 and 3, which gives strict qualifications for men teaching the Bible, as well as strict instructions that women should not teach adult men. We were just organizing the material that the church pumped out to us to give them. We would organize lots of social outings for the group and we did many projects for the community, feeding the homeless, doing one day mission events, writing the soldiers overseas and other events but nothing was about the Gospel. Not once did we biblically witness to a lost person, because we ourselves were lost. What a time of total deception we were under. However, we don't regret any of it because we know the Lord was using every bit of it to bring about the moment we are in now, exposing this movement to you, the reader.

In addition to this, we recently had an encounter at another very popular seeker style church. This past fall we were at a sound biblical seminar in the Fort Worth area and decided to go see how they were doing church at Ed Young Jr.'s Fellowship Church in Grapevine Texas. To no shock of our own it was very reminiscent of LifeChurch's look and feel. As we pulled into the drive of the mega facility, men standing out in the rain with fluorescent vests pointed us onward to the VIP parking for visitors. It was an effortless entry and they made you feel important with all the VIP signs especially because you were a visitor. As we walked into the place it was once again the loft style feel with the industrial style fixtures and lots of hustle and bustle. We were in between "experiences" so people were coming and going out of the doors. Instantly we had smiley people coming at us with bulletins and fingers pointing to the visitor's center. We stuck out like a sore thumb because Vince normally wears a suit and Lori in a modest dress. That is definitely not the norm, there is no rule on how to dress at church, but come on, if you can dress up for a date, can we not at least give the Lord the same attention. So there we were in the midst of the hub and we see promo posters everywhere for all their hip and groovy conferences they have planned just for *you*! (They were even on the bathroom stalls) Right dead center when you walked in there was a huge almost floor to ceiling promo for the next series "Run to the House" where Rev Run from the 80's rap group RUN DMC would be speaking. That was apparently the big push that week, all the host team members had their "Run to the House" shirts on with jeans to give serious PR to the following weeks.

As we entered into the visitor's center, everyone was very friendly, the coffee bar was going, the music was rockin' and the place was hoppin'. A guy who literally comes out of nowhere asks if we're new to the joint and wants to give us some freebies. We are curious as to what they are handing out to people so we take one. It's a big orange bag, eco-friendly material, filled with a t-shirt that has a giant shark on it and says "Shark Weak" across it. Apparently a few weeks before that had been the big series, playing off of the popular series from the Discovery Channel and having the star from Soul Surfer be a featured guest at the experiences. Included with our ridiculous shirts was a dvd of shark weak and also a cd of the same sermon preached on the topic. Among that we had a visitors booklet and a pink bracelet that had a catchy women's power slogan on it. (just what every guy wants as a new visitor for a welcome gift) So they talk to us for a bit and tell us to hurry on in for the next show.

It was already starting as we made our way in. It was so loud and very dark in there that Lori was having flashbacks to the pagan days of concert attending of some of the loudest bands. There were people with a way to see down the aisles and you had to shout to them "there's two of us!" They quickly wanted us to get a great seat up front, but we opted for the side middle just to not be blasted with the volume. As we make our way into our movie theatre style seat we both were a bit in shock. The "worship team" on stage was filled with the shiniest and pretty people. They too were decked out in their skinny jeans and Abercrombie and Fitch attire.

It was hard to see past all of that to hear the content of the songs, but the lyrics were very ethereal and catchy. You had a choir in the corner made up of about 20-25 people dancing and jammin', helping to whip the crowd up along with your lead vocals. It was quite the show. They did about three songs and a solo of a secular song "Personal Jesus" and had the lead singers showcase their skills. We were shocked as they did that song because the roots of it are very bad. Before this book we didn't know all of the following information until further research. The inspiration of the song was from the book Elvis and Me by Priscilla Presley. According to songwriter Martin Gore: "It's a song about being a Jesus for somebody else, someone to give you hope and care. It's about how Elvis was her man and her mentor and how often that happens in love relationships; how everybody's heart is like a god in some way, and that's not a very balanced view of someone, is it." (7) Let's keep in mind that Marilyn Manson also did a cover of this song in 2004 and it was the lead single on that album. And this was the song that Fellowship Church decided to do as a solo when everyone was sitting down getting ready to prepare for the sermon. Are you kidding? If that doesn't make you stop and think, it should. Consider the sources of where this song came from and they are now singing their hearts out to it to prepare you to hear from God's word. It is really sickening and an utter slap in the face of a Holy God.

Then a speaker came out. Ed Young Jr was not there the day we attended, so we got to hear a relevant story-at least that is what we'll call it- rather than a sermon. The guy comes out and tells of anecdotes of his kids, relates that back to life, throws in some verses for good measure about three fourths of the way into the "sermon." He inserts a lot of humor and jokes then ties up with a challenge and a prayer for everyone. There was no Gospel. Not even a hint of it. If you were a lost person there, which I'm sure there were many, you had no way of knowing how your sins could be forgiven. They have another staff member come out, do some witty banter, throw in some promos for the rev run series and how you can get plugged into the Fellowship Family. Then it is all over as fast as it started. They play a song to lead you out of the experience and it all literally happens in just at an hour.

We decided to go back into the coffee house to talk to someone. We were somehow divinely at the right time because the guy that came on stage was in there. Lori was casually walking around looking at the material being sold in the shop and most of it was all of Ed's series on CD and DVD format as well as their books. One of the more shocking items was apparently a series Ed did on The Twilight books and movies, of which a Mormon female wrote those books. We personally have not seen or heard that series he did so we don't want to comment on the content of them, but just by packaging something that looks identical to the Twilight book covers is again playing on the whole relevant idea of giving the seeking people what they want and what they will recognize to draw them in. Vince goes up to him and explains that we are visitors and when asked "how did we like it?" Vince said something to the effect of, "I have a question that is more of a concern; we just came from the last service and I didn't hear the Gospel . . ." The answer we were given was, that the speaker might not have talked about it directly today, but it's central in everything they do there at Fellowship Church. He also mentioned a booklet in the backs of the chairs that show and explain the Gospel, so someone can come to know about it that way (we read that booklet, and there was no Biblical gospel there, either). The man went on to say that the Gospel was touched on, just not directly hit that Sunday in particular, and not to judge them based just on that one Sunday. Vince reminded him that there was not only no gospel, but no mention of sin of any degree, and you have to understand sin for the gospel to make sense. The man kept referring back to the gospel supposedly being central to everything they do there, and continued to refer back to that booklet. Basically give it another shot; Lori then says, "How do you know that you are not turning out false converts?" It appeared the gentleman didn't know what that term meant. He says, "How do you mean?" and Lori then proceeds with asking him how do you know that the people you are baptizing (which they offer directly at the place on any Sunday so you can get baptized right after you have just gotten saved) have truly become Christians? So he again proceeds to say, well they read the booklet and someone would go over that booklet with them. Lori asked, "so you guys are counting on the fact that a new or lost person is going to know to pick up that booklet and then read it and therefore get saved that way rather than you preaching it from the pulpit?" The guy basically agreed to that idea and was started to get a little bit uncomfortable. He said they have a new members orientation that goes over those facts too. We, and him, were very cordial and kind during the conversation and we had received our answers. We saw what was going on at this place. It did not represent Christ in any way. Lori left him with a gentle word of caution by saying "be careful with this type of seeker style church, it is very easy to turn out false converts in this setting and it can be dangerous. We are, in fact, truly saved, but there are many back in that setting that are not. Just be careful with what you are doing here." Vince shook his hand and said "Thanks for your time, just wish I would have heard the Gospel today." It was simply very sad to see yet another seeker-friendly church trying to entertain unbelievers, and even that without the Gospel.

We want you and others to know how dangerous the seeker movement can be and how you might have been duped into believing you are saved, when most likely the majority of the members at seeker churches are no different than we were. People cannot be saved unless they first hear the Gospel (Romans 10:17), which we never heard at Lifechurch.

Galatations 1:8
But even if we, or an angel from heaven, should preach to you a gospel contrary to what we have preached to you, he is to be accursed!

In summation, the seeker-driven message that people are told to follow is basically something like "God, You'll have to show ME what Jesus can do for ME if You want to have a relationship with ME."

2 Corinthians 4:5
"For we do not preach ourselves but Christ Jesus as Lord, and ourselves as your bond-servants for Jesus' sake." *(emphasis added)*

Romans 16:17-18
"Now I urge you, brethren, keep your eye on those who cause dissentions and hindrances contrary to the teaching which you learned, and turn away from them. For such men are slaves, not of our Lord Christ but of their own appetites; and by their smooth and flattering speech they deceive the hearts of the unsuspecting." *(emphasis added)*

1 Corinthians 1:18-25, 27
"For the word of the cross is foolishness to those who are perishing, but to us who are being saved it is the power of God. For it is written, 'I will destroy the wisdom of the wise, and the cleverness of the clever I will set aside.' Where is the wise man? Where is the scribe? Where is the debater of this age? Has not God made foolish the wisdom of the world through its wisdom did not come to know God, God was well-pleased through the foolishness of the message preached to save those who believe. For indeed Jews ask for signs and Greeks search for wisdom; but we preach Christ crucified, to Jews a stumbling block and to Gentiles foolishness, but to those who are the called, both Jews and Greeks, Christ the power of God and the wisdom of Go. Because the foolishness of God is wiser than men, and the weakness of God is stronger than men."

"but God has chosen the foolish things of the world to shame the wise, and God has chosen the weak things of the world to shame the things which are strong."

1 Corinthians 2:14
"But a natural man does not accept the things of the Spirit of God, for they are foolishness to him and he cannot understand them, because they are spiritually appraised."

Falsified

The Lord, by His Sovereign hand, brought about something wonderful out of LifeChurch - meeting one another. I (Lori) did know in my heart that Vince was the man the Lord had picked out for me, I just had no idea what a refining process He was going to do through us and in us by saving us both radically early in our marriage.

In the next chapter we will briefly look through the lens of Scripture about how church should be done.

Chapter 3

The Biblical Approach to Church

"They were continually devoting themselves to the apostles' teaching and to fellowship, to the breaking of bread and to prayer." Acts 2:42

"Until I come, give attention to the public reading of Scripture, to exhortation and teaching." 1Timothy 4:13

Take pains with these things; be absorbed in them, so that your progress will be evident to all. Pay close attention to yourself and to your teaching; persevere in these things, for as you do this you will ensure salvation both for yourself and for those who hear you." 1 Timothy 4:15-16

We have looked at how church is being done in most modern day churches currently to appeal to the needs of the un-churched. Church biblically should be focusing on the edification of the body of believers and the preaching of the Word. Lets take a minute to stop and see how the Word of God portrays the essentials of the church.

2 Timothy 3:16-17
"All Scripture is breathed out by God and profitable for teaching, for reproof, for correction, for training in righteousness so

the man of God may be adequate, equipped for every good work." (ESV)

The words of the Lord were essentially breathed out from Him through the use of the writers of the Bible. He used their minds, vocabularies and experiences to produce His infallible perfect and inerrant word. (8)

We do not have the liberty to just make up how we want to do church and how we want to appeal to the masses, we have direct and clear guidance from the Lord on this topic. Many today in church leadership are seeking those who are of the world, rather than those who are true children of God and in the world. Remember church was originally designed for those who are saved and to build them up to go out into the world and proclaim the good news to the lost. However, we have gotten that pattern reversed today and we are doing church for the lost people and bringing them into the fold. Why do you think the church now no longer looks different from the world? Because there is no distinction, the lost are being entertained by church now. We have completely lost sight of the origins of what the Lord gave us as an example.

Pastor Mark Dever explains this concept more clearly, "Jesus established the church to be a public, earthly institution that would mark out, affirm, and oversee those who profess to believe in him (*Matt. 16:18-19, 18:15-20*). Jesus established the church to publicly declare those who belong to Him in order to give the world a display of the good news about Himself (*John 17:21, 23*; see also *Eph. 3:10*). Jesus wants the world to know who belongs to Him and who doesn't. And how is the world to know who belongs to Him and who doesn't? They are to see which people publicly identify themselves with His people in the visible, public institution He established for this very purpose. They're to look at the members of His church. And if some people claim to be part of the universal church even though they belong to no local church, they reject Jesus' plan for them and his church. Jesus intends for His people to be marked out as a visible, public group, which means joining together in local churches. (9)

The church is designed to practice church discipline (Matthew 19: 15-20), to teach, to edify, and equip the believers to go out into the entire world and fulfill the Great Commission (Matthew 28: 18-20, Mark 16:15), how then are the people to do these things if they are not saved? By not following a biblical approach to church, all of these commands get confused and distorted. Rather than going out into all the world to preach the good news of Christ crucified and resurrected, they end up going out to do community projects and spread the social gospel of good works. Community projects are not bad, but if we are just clothing the homeless but not telling them they are going to hell without Christ, what good have we done? If we simply put a jacket on their back and food in their bowl and we don't ever tell them about their lost soul and their need of a Savior, what good is saving a life on earth if we are not telling them how to inherit eternal life after this one? The social gospel will not save people. It merely helps people here on earth with monetary needs. The Gospel of Jesus Christ is about saving souls for eternity. There is a huge distinction there. We should be showing them their need for a Savior through the law (ten commandments) and then the Gospel, thus caring for their souls first then caring for their earthly needs. When we get away from the biblical model for church on earth you can begin to see where the trickle down effect comes into play and this is only one example.

The main distortion happening today in churches is getting away from the clear teaching on the role of the Pastor in the church. For example, the scriptures say,

> 1 Timothy 6:3-4
> *"If anyone advocates a different doctrine and does not agree with sound words, those of our Lord Jesus Christ, and with the doctrine conforming to godliness, he is conceited and understands nothing; but he has a morbid interest in controversial questions and disputes about words, out of which arise envy, strife, abusive language, evil suspicions."*

2 Timothy 2:15-16

> "Be diligent to present yourself approved to God as a workman who does not need to be ashamed, accurately handling the word of truth. But avoid worldly and empty chatter, for it will lead to further ungodliness."

1 Timothy 3: 1-7

> "It is a trustworthy statement: if any man aspires to the office overseer, it is a fine work he desires to do. An overseer, the, must be above reproach, the husband of one wife, temperate, prudent, respectable, hospitable, able to teach, not addicted to wine or pugnacious, but gentle, peaceable, free from the love of money. He must be one who manages his own household well, keeping his children under control with all dignity (but if a man does not know how to manage his own household, how will he take care of the church of God?) and not a new convert so that he will not become conceited and fall into the condemnation incurred by the devil. And he must have a good reputation with those outside the church, so that he will not fall into reproach and the snare of the devil."

These verses here are prime examples of what the office of Pastoral shepherding should look like. He is to be careful with the word, expositing it correctly and accurately handling the word. He should not be drawing out his own conclusions from a passage incorrectly.

The Pastor is to be someone that is above reproach and not full of empty chatter as mentioned above in scripture. That is all we seem to see on television interviews now are these mega church pastors engaging in silly talk or not being able to provide clear concise answers that are clearly found in scripture.

In conclusion, the biblical method of church is not something to be ignored, to be watered down or with which to be toyed. God's word is very clear on how church is to be done and there are reasons for it as we have discussed. The church is to remain pure, and a portrait of the bride of Christ, not full of distractions and silliness.

Chapter 4

An Eye Opening Experience on Hollywood Blvd

We've all seen the glitz and glamour of Hollywood on television. We've seen the famous Hollywood Walk of Fame and the hoopla of when a celebrity gets their name on a star. That's the goal of what each actor is striving for when they try to go there to make it big. They know they have "arrived" when their name appears on a sidewalk outlined by a star. This too of course is on the agenda of every tourist that comes to Hollywood, to see Hollywood Boulevard and walk along the star studded sidewalk trying to find their favorite among the masses.

We had the opportunity to go to California recently and we basically tried to steer clear of the typical tourist sites, however we did end up on Hollywood Boulevard by accident of sorts when trying to search out the Church of Scientology for witnessing purposes. What we came across was more than shocking- it was disturbing and filthy. Most of all, it was heartbreaking. We did not quite realize where we were until looking down the street and realizing . . . "oh, this is Hollywood Boulevard,. . . . this is it???" The reason we had this reaction was because at first glance it looked like every other street, which is until you look out the window and see these dingy stars on a sidewalk. Then you start to see the tour buses of "Hollywood Celebrity Home Tours." As we drove a little further we see the famous Pantages Theater, again, it was nothing fancy, nothing stood out about it and it looked like a hole in the wall. We could not believe all the hype that we have heard surrounding Hollywood Boulevard and all the "cool" things to see there. It was nothing but a farce. A facade. A mask of television and movies stripped down to a dirty sidewalk with dirty shops and ordinary people trying to pretend to be extraordinary. It was exactly what the world is everywhere; lost, broken people trying to find their place in society, all with broken dreams and a lost soul inside. It was heartbreaking because here is a place that is supposed to be the epitome of glamour "where all your dreams come true", and it was reduced to nothing more than trashy skewed versions of the supposed American dream.

All that kept coming to our minds as we saw the crowds of people on either side of the street, was that these people were so lost and bound for eternal destruction if nobody ever intervenes with the Gospel. We are not referring to the one you hear at your local seeker friendly church. America is a great mission field in and of itself, but Hollywood Boulevard is definitely the hub of that field. It is a hub of lies. It was just a simple but stern reminder of the urgent need to spread the Gospel wherever we are. We give a great deal of credit to the Living Waters Ministry team because they are actively doing street witnessing down there in California on a regular basis.

Driving down Hollywood Boulevard was a very eye opening experience in the sense that we both had an overwhelming burden for the lost, and yet at the same time you had to guard your own heart and mind from the filth that surrounds and invades every square inch that you look on the Boulevard. We want to take this chapter to just remind believers that are reading this book to pray for those that witness in that mission field of the Boulevard, its not an easy task, but one that those down there are doing and one that we are commanded to do in our neighborhoods and cities.

Hollywood was a very clear reminder that nothing you see and hear is as it seems, it pulled the veil off of an idea that's been birthed into people's minds that the "grass is greener" over there. This idea has been going on since the beginning of time back in Eden where the serpent told man that he could be like God. The Hollywood wannabes not only wants to be like God, but in a sense want to be a god. They want to be in charge of their own destiny using Hollywood as a springboard to get there. Hollywood doesn't love them any more than the serpent loved Adam and Eve. Hollywood wants money, and will use any willing soul to get it. Again, its all a façade being masqueraded as reality and people are buying into it left and right. They too are eating the fruit as fast as they can. Remember the words of Paul when he said,

> "Not that I speak from want, for I have learned to be content in whatever circumstances I am." (Philippians 4:11, emphasis added)

Matthew also talks about gaining the world versus losing your soul:

> "For what will it profit a man if he gains the whole world and forfeits his soul? Or what will a man give in exchange for his soul?" (see also Mark 8:36 and Luke 9:25)

All this simply, and sadly, goes back to a false gospel - a lie - being spread like gangrene across the country and around the world. It's a fake gospel that doesn't tell people that there's more to life than fame and fortune and Hollywood being just one example. A gospel that tells people they can have their best life *now*. Therefore, because many people are told a false gospel, there are masses of people within Christianity that *think* they are saved, and are being *told* they are saved, but are actually victims of false conversion.

Chapter 5

Evangelism: The Great Commission & Commandment

"And He said to them, 'Go into all the world and preach the gospel to all creation." Mark 16:15

"Do you consider yourself to be a good person?" (10) This is how evangelist Ray Comfort starts his dialogue with the lost people of the world. Evangelism is a topic that either makes Christians uncomfortable or zealous to do. The television program "Way of the Master" has been an extremely helpful tool to us and to Lori's conversion of how to learn effective and biblical evangelism. Its evangelism the way Jesus did. We are called to go into all the world and preach the Gospel. Two different direct times in the Gospels, we have this very command from Jesus.

Matthew 28:19-20
"Go therefore and make disciples of all the nations, baptizing them in the name of the Father and the Son and of the Holy Spirit, teaching them to observe all that I commanded you."

Ray Comfort talks about when he first started obeying this commandment, "I had an itinerant ministry, and heard pastors say things like, 'we had a series of meetings last month. There were eighty converts, and I cant find even one in my church.' My frustration was added to because the Church in general didn't even seem interested in reaching the lost. It had as much attraction to the word 'evangelism' as the world has to the word 'righteousness;'" (11)

This is the problem with the modern day evangelism; Christians in particular are the most dangerous at it. They will say things like, "Are you saved? Do you know Jesus? There is a God-shaped hole in your heart that only Jesus can fill!" They are not pointing lost people to their sin first, they are just telling them to ask for forgiveness, that's the problem, people don't know what they are asking forgiveness for. This is what cranks out the false conversions because people are not equipped to biblically evangelize to the lost in a way that pricks the conscience and shows them the need for a Savior.

Comfort says, "Do you enjoy worshiping God? Most people in the Church would say they do. Every Sunday all across the country, auditoriums are filled with hand-raising, God-loving Christians singing their praises to God. That's understandable, because when the Holy Spirit dwells within us, it's not hard to worship our Creator. In the light of the Cross, it's as natural to worship God as it is for flowers to open their petals in the warm sunlight. May I ask you a personal question? When was the last time you shared your faith with an unsaved person?" Comfort states, "We have been gazing to the heavens while sinners are sinking into Hell." (11)

That is a very poignant statement Comfort makes, think about that, we as Christians claim to love the Lord so much and have our eyes fixed on Him, while all around us our loved ones, co-workers, neighbors, and friends are going to hell and we have the answer. What a selfish way to live life, knowing you have the cure or the answer to the biggest question in life and you don't share it for what reason? Fear? Embarrassment? Anxiety? These are not good reasons. If you are getting ready to go on a roller coaster, you have fear, but you do it anyway. If you are climbing the corporate ladder and you have to give a speech in front of a crowd, you might be worried about being embarrassed in front of a group, but you do it anyway. You have to go to the dentist for a toothache, you have anxiety, but you do it anyway. These are all situations where the same emotions creep in, but what's the difference in following through with those situations versus evangelism? Answer . . . the motive. The motive in all three scenarios above is for you. When it's all about you, of course you'll go through the uncomfortable emotions and thought processes because you have something to gain in the picture. However, when it comes to evangelism its about someone else, therefore you can afford to be lazy. On the contrary reader, you cannot. If you are soundly saved, you have the obligation and the responsibility just as much to that lost person as you do to yourself in a selfish motive situation. As Comfort and Kirk Cameron have often said on their program Way of the Master, its as if there is a burning building and we know people are inside, we run to them to grab them out of the fire, we don't wait until the opportunity or mood is right. Lives are at stake, souls forever will perish if we don't intervene and share the good news of the Gospel.

You might be saying, well how do I cross over from the earthly conversations into the spiritual realm? Again, the team at Living Waters and other biblical ministries out there has come up with some very good icebreakers of sorts to accomplish just that. We were never used to be people that handed out tracts, but thanks to the creativity of people like Comfort, we have found people will end up asking us for more gospel tracts. Living Waters has a very popular "Million Dollar Bill Tract" that looks like real money and has the gospel on the back of it. You simply ask a person something like this, "have you seen one of these?" or my (Lori) favorite expression especially when leaving restaurants is to stop by the table quickly and politely and say "Have you gotten your million today?" You just lay it on the table, smile and walk off. Its simple, easy, and you've left them with the gospel message over a dinner conversation. One of the most interesting settings is to do it when you are leaving a restaurant, especially one that is crowded and many people are waiting on tables and you have a ton of people just standing there, bored, idle, and prime opportunities for a gospel tract. We will hand them out as we have finished our meal to the hungry patrons and say here's a million for ya, hand them out to the people quickly and then leave. Again, another great opportunity where people will take the time to read it, hopefully engage with each other and we allow the Holy Spirit to do the work through the tract. This is an easy way to get started if you are uncomfortable witnessing directly but want to start getting the message out there. (See the Tips on Tracting section in the back of the book for more creative ways to spread the Gospel.)

Another creative way to witness and get the tract out was pointed out by a friend on her website, www.fishwithtrish.com, Trisha Ramos came up with the fast food drive thru tract encounter. You simply take two tracts, pull up the window to pay and ask to pay for the person behind you. You then ask the employee to give the tract to the person and then give the other tract to the employee so they know why you are doing this "kind thing" in the eyes of the world, to share the truth. Not just to make their day or do a good work. But it's a means to get the gospel out there. To watch a video of Trish doing this visit her website and you can see exactly what it looks like.

The key to handing out tracts is to just do it. The tract does all the work for you, so by getting creative in handing them out, it becomes a bit of challenge and evangelism actually starts turning into something fun to do and not something scary. Equip yourself in the word so that you can effectively share the gospel with people. Carry tracts as a bridge-way into the conversation.

Dear reader, if you are a fellow Christian, this command from our Lord to go into all the world to preach the gospel is just that – a Command. It is not an option He gave to us. It is not something we can read over and think "It's just not for me" or other similar excuses. This is a direct command given to us by our Lord and we are expected to follow it. We actually do have two options. We can directly and willfully choose to disobey our Lord, or we can choose to directly obey our Lord. There is no in-between. There is no gray. People are all around you: across the street, next door, in your workplace, in your local grocery store – maybe even your own home. Maybe you have a family member who is not saved. Think of all the people, the ones you know personally who are not saved, from each of those places I just mentioned. Think of where they will spend eternity if they were to die tonight. As Lori said before, you have the cure for their sin disease, the cure that could change their *eternity*, and you are keeping that cure from them. Friends, that is mean. That is *really* mean.

We beg you, if you know someone who would be going straight to hell if they were to die at this very moment, please give them the cure. Even if they reject the cure, you will still have been faithful in your obedience to our Lord, to our Savior.

Chapter 6

Word of Faith & The Prosperity Gospel

"For there are many rebellious men, empty talkers and deceivers, especially those of the circumcision, who must be silenced because they are upsetting whole families, teaching things they should not teach for the sake of sordid gain." Titus 1:10-11

"They profess to know God, but by their deeds they deny Him, being detestable and disobedient and worthless for any good deed." Titus 1:16

"For certain persons have crept in unnoticed, those who were long beforehand marked out for this condemnation, ungodly persons who turn the grace of God into licentiousness and deny our only Master and Lord, Jesus Christ." Jude 1:4

This chapter will be somewhat brief, but is necessary for the topic of false conversion. TV preachers are very slick, and the majority of them are leading masses astray, supposedly using Scripture to back up their claims. Men and women are on national and worldwide television "preaching" that God wants everyone to always be healthy and wealthy therefore resulting in prosperity in

Falsified

all things, all the time. Many of them teach that we are actually "little gods" because, after all, we were created in the image of God. Some actually going as far as to say that we *are* everything God is and was and ever will be. Most of them claim to able to physically heal people, cast out demons, make futuristic prophecies (most prophecies of which have never happened). Some claim to have taken trips to Heaven and back, receive direct and extra-Biblical revelations from God, and even supposedly had personal conversations with God. As the verses at the beginning of this chapter say, these "preachers" profess to know God, but deny Him by what they do. They are deceivers who should not teach but do so for one reason and one reason alone. Money.

    Lori was duped by two of these false teachers, Joel Osteen and Joyce Meyer. Two of the lesser recognized false teachers, especially amongst evangelical Christians. I went through a time where I was sick, nothing life threatening but was a season of life where illness did plague the body for the good part of a year. I fell into the trap of watching Joel Osteen every Tuesday night and reading his book. I bought into the lie of if I just quoted to myself that "I am a victor and not a victim" that I would start to overcome this illness eventually. I would continually do self-affirmations that Joel was pumping at me from the television screen, all the while living in total rebellion to my Lord. I had no real understanding of God's sovereignty and that possibly the reason I was sick was that it was the work of God in my life for a reason. That thought never crossed into my mind. I heard over and over that God doesn't want us to be sick and miserable, but that He wants us to live a victorious life. Had I been into the word of God I would of quickly realized this wasn't lining up with the life of the apostles at all and those men were hand picked by the Lord. Their lives got worse as it went on, they were persecuted, they were homeless, poor, in prison, and yet they were blessed and cared for. These were the truths I needed to be rooted in, yet I wasn't. I was busy letting a self help guru on the screen tell me that I was going to feel better if I just believed enough. Where is there any valid Scripture that backs that up? There isn't. We are not promised a good and easy life on this side of eternity, but we are promised in Matthew 28:20 that "lo, I am with you always even to the end of the age."

After the Lord eventually healed me over time, nothing that I did obviously, I turned to another false teacher unknowingly. This time not only was truth being twisted but it was from an authority who was not even fit to be teaching, Joyce Meyer. We've already addressed that women acting as pastors as defined in 1 Timothy 3:2 are not to be exercising the authority of that role.

Titus 1:6 states clearly the qualifications of a pastor, see below the text and how a woman cannot fit into this criteria for the office of pastor:

> "namely, if any man is above reproach, the husband of one wife, having children who believe, not accused of dissipation or rebellion."

I used to watch Joyce Meyer every morning before I was saved and feed on her quick wit and sassy style. I used to think, "she is just telling it like it is!" I remember thinking her "sermons" on the battle in your mind were just phenomenal. She was telling me how to just get over it and move on. It was a much starker difference than Joel. Joel was happy and feel good, Joyce was no-nonsense no frills just cut to the core motivation. She was teaching a false gospel of the little gods lesson as Vince mentioned above. I had emailed asking for prayer during that time and not but a few weeks later did I get things in the mail from her ministry basically forcing an "offering" and that in order to continue being blessed, I needed to return money in the envelope that was sent. That happened repeatedly until I moved from that address. Many women who love that strong willed nature in a female buy into Joyce Meyer and all that she is selling. That is not the character of a godly woman, which I will address later on in the book.

Vince never really had any interest in most of the TV preachers. I never watched much TV anyway. I did watch some of the more minor, non-heretical, not as popular teachers, but I never got into Joel Osteen, TD Jakes, Benny Hinn, Jesse Duplantis, or any of the other heretics on TV. However, before God graciously saved me, I could have watched them and probably would not have given much thought to it. I probably would have thought some of it was strange . . . but heresy? I didn't even know the word "heresy" existed until a couple of years ago. I surely did not know how deep and dark their teaching really goes, and how especially evil these men and women really are. Justin Peters and his ministry really opened my eyes to most of that.

This movement is not only dangerous to the souls of many who are being falsely converted, but who are also being led in universal communions. We were witness to this concept at a Benny Hinn Crusade in Dallas, Texas in September. People were coming down the aisle in droves to get saved and then were led in a universalistic communion. They were not told to examine themselves in light of scripture in the biblical sense; it was completely twisted into believing that if you took the sacraments it would heal you from within. Dangerous beyond words. There was a two-fold problem with this event, turning out false converts and then in the next minute leading them into communion that was not understood in the purest sense. This movement is sweeping the nation and the world and people are so hungry for "something more" in their lives, they buy into this culture of health, wealth, and even fame for the exchange of all that they have. Among those already listed, a few of the other more well known television preachers supporting this movement are as follows: Kenneth and Gloria Copeland, Creflo Dollar, T.D. Jakes, Paula White, Jesse Duplantis and several others.

Speaking of Jesse Duplantis we also got the opportunity to hear him in person in the midst of writing this book. In one word to describe what we saw would be "circus." This man is a false prophet to the core. He blasphemed the name of God 23 times in an hour. He preached on the passage of the 23rd Psalm and we have never seen it butchered any more than at that moment. He spoke on off color topics that are too vulgar to even mention in this book. We will just run down a list of quotes that he directly said and you be the judge and test it against scripture and see for yourself:

- "Jesus never explained the gospel himself, he didn't have enough time, he was only here for 30 years."
- "I create my world and I walk in it. It's my world."- this is in response to his daughter saying nothing seems to affect you.
- "I tried it and didn't like it." –in response to being sick
- "God never told us to come together in the unity of doctrine."
- "Women like Esau"
- "I preach on the God of Abraham, Issaac, and Jacob. That is wrong, it should have been Abraham, Issac and Esau." –in talking about the lineage (basically calling God a liar because he didn't like how the lineup goes in the Bible)
- "The devil has made the church believe that poverty is a blessing. Anyone with common sense knows it's a curse."
- "He make you slippery when the devil is trying to get you." –in reference to anointing my head with oil verse of Psalm 23:5.
- "I'm not afraid to die." "I wanna go for that ride"-in reference to talking about the rapture.
- "Heaven is a wonderful place because there is no money there." Why is everyone so happy in heaven, "Because everyone has what they want."

Then to close the service, a lengthy time is spent on giving money so that you can be blessed back financially 30, 60, or 100 fold. He proceeds to tell the congregation that he has signed a contract in Europe to go on the atheist network. "They think I'm a comedian." So he wants to turn in that check of 50,000 to the network the next day so he can "give the devil a black eye on

Halloween." It was utterly ridiculous and totally blasphemous to our God. At the end of his "sermon", he states his calling in life is "to preach and teach the un-compromised Word of God."

After reading the quotes and summary of the service . . . . you decide if he's fulfilling that mission or if there is another agenda going on there. There were many there giving lots of money to Mr. Duplantis and sowing their seed of harvest while agreeing with him all the way to heresy land. It was vile and sad all at the same time. More false conversion as he led people into a sinner's prayer and once again, another day for victims to fall prey to a wolf in sheep's clothing. And just like every other word of faith preacher, he mentioned that people should be healed through the broken then resurrected body of Christ. He too spoke on just having enough faith and you too can be prosperous in every way.

The expert on this topic would be the ministry of Justin Peters. He is a man that has gone around exposing and has an entire ministry based on educating people as to what the Word of Faith teachers are doing. For more in depth study of this topic please visit Justin's website as noted in the back of the book.

Again, we touch on this area because so many are being led into false conversion, its not just the seeker churches that are very good at this, the Word of Faith movement is also very stellar at it as well. By telling people a false gospel, people are getting falsely converted, so we felt it best to address this topic. Again this is an easy way that satan has used and is currently using to lead masses of people away from the Biblical Gospel.

Chapter 7

Hypocrisy Vs. Living the Word

> *"Woe to you, scribes and Pharisees, hypocrites! For you are like whitewashed tombs, which on the outside appear beautiful, but inside they are full of dead men's bones and all uncleanness. So you, too, outwardly appear righteous to men, but inwardly you are full of hypocrisy and lawlessness." Matthew 23:27-28*

Hypocrisy is rampant. People are claiming the name of Christ, but denying Him by their lifestyle. More simply put, these people have no fruit in keeping with repentance (Matthew 3:8). This is a direct result of false conversion, which in turn is a direct result of God's Word and the Biblical Gospel being abandoned in most Christian churches worldwide.

> *John 14:15 says,*
> *"If you love me, you will keep my commandments."*

Growing up in the Christian church, I (Vince) sadly never heard the Biblical gospel, or at least I don't remember hearing it. My life makes perfect sense to me now because I know the Truth, and it has set me free (John 8:32). It has set me free because the

Holy Spirit now resides in me, and He has given me a new heart with new desires. I used to be a huge hypocrite. I only practiced what I preached half the time. Praise be to the Lord that He did eventually reveal to me my true wicked self, and saved me from myself.

When people hear Gospel-less preaching from the pulpit, or if they always hear that they have to "do this" or "do that" for Jesus in order for Him to be pleased with them, that will ultimately lead people to think that the source of Christianity is good works, this leading to false conversion. People *cannot* do *anything* to please God apart from a heart that has been regenerated by the Holy Spirit. The result is people inevitably and eventually failing to grow in holiness – to look more like Christ. Hypocrisy is a branch of false conversion.

Strangely but not surprisingly, people still talk about how the Bible says to approach life, but will continually fail to live it out themselves. They talk about how things should be done, referencing the Bible, but never actually obeying the Scriptures. The best example of this from the text is the Pharisees as talked about in Matthew 23: 1-33. The Pharisees thought they were such good people because they knew the Law of God like the back of their hand. However, they failed to live it out. They did not practice what they preached. In fact, it was impossible for them to do so because their hearts were still at enmity with God. Jesus hated their hypocrisy so much the he pronounced seven consecutive "woes" upon them. They talked about obeying the Law, but never told people the Gospel. They never understood that obeying God's laws are impossible without Christ. Without a regenerated heart that can only come from obedience to the Gospel.

None of us will ever reach perfectionism before God calls us home, but by the power of the Holy Spirit we can be consistently moving in that direction. 1 John actually gives us signs that we can look for in our own lives to determine if we are living the Word, and growing in holiness to be more like Christ.

> *1 John 2:15 says,*
> *"Do not love the world nor the things in the world. If anyone loves the world, the love of the Father is not in him."*

We are not talking about reaching perfection as living without sin in this life, but rather a difference in direction. We don't dive into sin once we are saved, we may fall into it on occasion but we don't do so willingly as we once did before conversion. The theological term for this is sanctification. Once we are born-again and God creates a new heart in us, the Holy Spirit, then residing in us starts the process of sanctification. Is there a decreasing pattern of sin in your life? Do you have the witness of the Holy Spirit in your life? Do you hate sin? Do you love the Word of God? These are some good questions to ask yourself.

> *I John 3:9 says,*
> *"No one who is born of God practices sin, because His seed abides in him; and he cannot sin, because he is born of God."*

God's word has everything we need for life and Godliness and the Holy Spirit uses His word to continually reveal to us sin in our lives. The word holiness literally means, "to set apart" or "set apart." Jesus repeatedly says that Christians should be different from the world. When the world sees us they should be noticing something different.

The danger of false conversion is hypocrisy. If you are falsely converted yet thinking you are saved, you are living a life contradictory to that of the Christian life. You are living a life of works based rather than that of allowing Christ to pay all of that penalty and therefore surrender to Him. Hypocrisy is something Lori used to say anytime someone would ask "what's your biggest pet peeve in life?" My standard answer, "a hypocrite." Oh the irony that I was one myself the whole time before I was saved. What's even scarier is that true Christians around me never once questioned my actions, my speech, or my dress. You would think that a person living in total rebellion yet calling themselves a child of God would result in some people saying "hey, something doesn't match up here." Not a one. True believers let me go about in my sin and confirmed me in it and said, oh she always is at church. Little did they know, my physical body was there but my soul couldn't of been further away from the Lord. If you are truly saved and you are reading this and you know of someone that is walking and living in total contradiction to that of a Christian's life, please talk to them gently and ask them how they justify the two lives. Revert back to the evangelism chapter, or just lead them through the Ten Commandments and show them how they've sinned against the Lord and let the law take effect on the proud heart.

If you are living in rebellion to Christ, and you are claiming to be His follower, you will always be living a double life. It's the only natural result you can produce. If your heart is not regenerated, and you are falsely converted, you will be living one life that looks good on the exterior for the world, and you will be living another one that pleases you and your father, the devil. The Holy Spirit cannot reside where unrepentant sin abounds. You live a double life, talk double speak, and therefore you do nothing but blaspheme the name of the Lord. You are lukewarm. As it says in Revelation 3:16, He will spit you out if you are neither hot nor cold.

Two words of caution, if you think you've been saved up to this point and you stop and look around and nothing sets you apart from the world, then, again, self examine yourself and see if you truly are in the faith. Remember I John 2: 19,

> 'They went out from us, but they were not really of us; for if they had been of us, they would have remained with us; but they went out, so that it would be shown that they all are not of us.'(emphasis ours)

Hypocrisy is too dangerous of a trap not to address it in this book. It is closely connected with false conversion, in your own life and that in the lives of others.

Chapter 8

Sin, Judgment, and Hell

Romans 6:23 "For the wages of sin is death, but the free gift of God is eternal life in Christ Jesus our Lord."

1 John 3:4 "Everyone who practices sin, also practices lawlessness; and sin is lawlessness."

Romans 3:23 "For all have sinned and fall short of the glory of God."

Sin entered the world through Adam and Eve, and this world has been under it's curse ever since. Romans 5:12 talks about death being spread to all men because all have sinned. Adam who was our federal representative was born into this world having not a single blemish of sin. However when he and Eve, in the garden, fell into sin from the temptation of the serpent, the world was never the same. From then on sin was present and it had to be dealt with. Spiritual death is the paycheck for every person's slavery to sin, says Dr. John MacArthur. This is a topic from which modern day pastors are steering clear because "sin" is just too "uncomfortable of a term to talk about." It makes people uneasy when they hear about their own wretched state. Pastors especially in the seeker friendly movement don't want an audience that will be anything less than entertained, and sin is not a very engaging topic. Most pastors want popularity and a big church. They want quantity not quality attendees and the topic of sin is not what brings them in by the droves. Talking about sin is not popular, at least not in today's society. The scriptures in Proverbs 20:6, say that every man will proclaim his own goodness. This statement is true. If you go out and ask a handful of people, "do you think you are good person?" they will usually respond with a confident "yes. However, Scripture says in Romans 3:12, there is none good, not even one." The outcome of false converts is typically that they have never looked at themselves as a sinner. They are too busy being told by these relevant pastors that God has a wonderful plan for their life instead of being told of their sin nature. This in and of itself is not only false, but therefore falsely convinces individuals into the belief that they are good. This is where they need to be taught of what is to come if they do not see their own sin.

Judgment

Judgment is the result of our sin. It is the recourse that must happen because a Holy and Just God created us. If there were not any judgment in this world all lawbreakers would be walking around free. Why do we even have rules if we are not going to follow them? The same principle applies to your eternal salvation. If we don't have a ruler of authority that is measuring our sin and therefore giving us what we deserve, what ordinance is there to anything?

> 2 Corinthians 5:10 says "For we must all appear before the judgment seat of Christ, so that each one may be recompensed for his deeds in the body according to what he has done whether good or bad."

It is clear in scripture that there will be a Day of Judgment and that you will have to face a Holy God. You will have to give an account of your life to Him on that day. Hebrews 9:27 talks about that it's appointed for men to die once and then come judgment. There is no way around that. We all will die one day and therefore you go to one of two places. We will explain the other place in a later chapter, but for now, we are dealing with the idea of false converts and all unsaved people. Judgment day is real. Hollywood has made the topic into movies and glossed over the real subject of what judgment day will look like. When you face the Lord upon your day of death, it will not be a movie, it will be real life and you will tremble at the amount of sin you truly have amassed when you come before a Holy God.

People here on earth want a just judgment for criminals who rape, murder, etc. however they are not willing to admit that they themselves are biblically guilty of the same crimes that the civil court punishes. You might say, "well I've never murdered someone, why should I be punished?"

I John 3:15 clearly says,

> "Everyone who hates his brother is a murderer; and you know that no murderer has eternal life abiding in him."

God is Holy and perfect and a just judge. Crimes against Him are stricter than even our civil court. Do you see the idea there? You are willing that a criminal be sent to jail forever, yet you yourself have done the same thing against a Holy God. This results in some form of judgment and payment for those sins . . . if you do not have Christ, that result is a wrath filled judgment.

> Acts 17:30 says "Therefore having overlooked the times of ignorance, God is now declaring to men that all people everywhere should repent because He has fixed a day in which He will judge the world in righteousness through a Man through he has appointed, having furnished proof to all men by raising Him from the dead."

HELL

> "Then He will also say to those on His left, 'depart from Me, accursed ones, into the eternal fire which has been prepared for the

> *devil and his angels. These will go away into eternal punishment but the righteous into eternal life." Matthew 25:41,46*

> *"And He will say, 'I tell you, I do not know where you are from; DEPART FROM ME, ALL YOU EVIL DOERS,' in that place there will be weeping and gnashing of teeth when you see Abraham and Isaac and Jacob and all the prophets in the kingdom of God but yourselves being thrown out." Luke 13:27-28*

Rob Bell is wrong. He may be confused and even sincere, but utterly wrong. We have spent time in heavy tears over Bell, pleading for God to show him the Truth, to bring him to repentance, and save him from himself and Hell. In his book "Love Wins", Rob Bell gives his version of hell, and from all the interviews that he's given on television (12) there is no real hell in his opinion, but rather hell is what you create for yourself, which is completely contrary to scripture. There is no gray on this subject. Jesus talked more about hell than He did heaven. Hell is eternal. It is forever. It is total separation from God, and an experience of the full wrath of God. It is a place where the worm never dies and the fire is not quenched as Mark 9:48 states. Think about that concept, total darkness, weeping and gnashing of teeth because the people there are still in rebellion toward the Lord and blaspheming His Name.

Hell is also another eternally important issue that you will not hear from many pastors today. They think the word hell is too offensive and would rather be popular, relevant and inviting than have you believe the truth, that you are a wretched person. This is where the danger creeps in. If a person is not told of the reality of hell, they are going to remain complacent in their view of the afterlife. Therefore, they will think they are saved but actually are victims of being falsely converted into the idea that they are "ok." This is exactly the point we were at and didn't even realize it. The seeker model church never openly told us of this reality. We barely even heard about sin, what sin is, and the eternal reality we would face if it were not dealt with. We lived our moral lives, wallowing in our sin, all the way being confirmed in it. We personally know of people who were openly living in fornication, the leaders of the seeker church knew about it, and allowed them to actively serve and lead in the church. There were others who were in an openly homosexual relationship that felt at ease there and enjoyed the "comfortable and non judgmental" atmosphere. These two situations literally make us weep because they are people we know, yet the reality of sin and hell was never brought before them to help them out of their falsely converted state. According to Scripture there is a biblical way that we are told to judge in the book of Luke, which is using Scripture itself to point out their sin in a loving but firm way. In both of the situations mentioned above, the individuals claimed to be Christians, therefore, according to Scripture that is the only biblical way you are allowed to judge these people. The fact that they are living immorally against the commandments of Scripture is of great concern. The greater concern is that they don't even realize they are not saved because they have not been confronted about their habitual sin (1 John 3:4-9)—and not just that particular sin—no sin was addressed. We were no different; we were of the same mindset not realizing how we were daily sinning against our Holy Lord. Our eyes were not opened, our hearts were not transformed, but the seeker church told us we were okay because we claimed to love Him and we believed in Jesus. The fact is we didn't truly love Him, nor did we believe in Him because we didn't obey His Word. We lived a life totally contradictory to His commands. We were hell bound in our moral Jesus loving state and the leaders of the church held our hand all the way into it.

As mentioned before, and clearly in Scripture, Hell is a real place. It is an eternal place. Even Hell glorifies God because His wrath is exemplified by sending unrepentant sinners there for punishment. This also reveals His righteous nature. It is a horrific, terrible, wrath-filled, empty, lonely, dark, evil, painful, torturing, unquenchable, unrelenting, fiery place of punishment for people who reject Christ, and His payment for sin, in this life.

That's the bad news.

But there's good news.

Chapter 9

The Gospel (or Good News) of Jesus Christ

"He made Him who knew no sin to be sin on our behalf, so that we might become the righteousness of God in Him." 2 Corinthians 5:21

"Being justified as a gift by His grace through the redemption which is in Christ Jesus." Romans 3:24

"For God so loved the world, that He sent His only begotten Son that none might perish but have everlasting life." John 3:16

"For the grace of God has appeared, bringing salvation to all men, instructing us to deny ungodliness and worldly desires and to live sensibly, righteously and godly in the present age, looking for the blessed hope and the appearing of the glory of our great God and Savior, Christ Jesus, who gave Himself for us to redeem us from every lawless deed, and to purify for Himself a people for His own possession, zealous for good deeds." Titus 2:11-14

Now we get to the greatest story ever told. The story and the news about the greatest Person Who ever walked on the face of this earth. It is AMAZING good news. To start off, here is a quote from one of our favorite pastors, Art Azurdia, in his sermon God saves Bad People, (13)

"God loves to save the most despicable kinds of people. And that's certainly true in my case. In getting me God wasn't getting something good. In getting me God wasn't getting anything special, in getting me God wasn't getting anything that would add to Him or benefit Him in any way, shape, or form. Have you forgotten by any chance the sewer out of which God rescued you? Which means, dear friends that our hope, our joy is grounded in this: that our God is absolutely relentless in his passionate pursuit to save sinners, not good people. God doesn't save good people; good people don't need to be saved. God saves bad people! Are you a bad person today? Then I am exceedingly glad that you are here, because that's what this congregation is, a congregation of bad people. Why do you come to this place? So that you can hear of the God Who saves bad people, Who loves bad people, Who rescues and delivers and extends mercy to bad people. Why bad people? Because doing so reveals the glory of His grace and the expansive boundaries of His love. Because doing so exposes the true potency of His saving accomplishments in His Son Jesus Christ. God loves to save bad people. We raise our fist in God's face and we say, "Why do You save some and not others?" And it makes us mad. In our arrogance it makes us mad. As the pot, we think we have rights to the Potter. "Why do You save some and not others?" And you understand of course the predisposition that's behind all of that: the assumption that we're all innocent. But when you understand as Rahab does that we are all guilty, then suddenly the amazing thing is not that God saves some and not others, the amazing thing is that God saves any! When you understand that we're all guilty, suddenly saving any becomes the most amazing display of the grace of God.

This is the Christian God. The God Who saves bad people. The God Who has revealed Himself to you most fully in Jesus Christ. The gracious God, the generous God, the warm-hearted God, the open-armed God, the God Who is for sinners! Are you a sinner? A sinner like Rahab, dominated by sin because of your enslavement to sin? The God of the Bible is full of power and full of love and eager to save. And He does so, dear friends, by the One Who is now come to us through the redeemed womanhood of Rahab, God's Own Son Jesus Christ. You are not beyond the reach of God's grace. It makes no difference, dear friend, how scandalous your sin may be; even if it's as ugly as that of Rahab's. Like Rahab, ask God to save you from death, and He will in ways far greater than you could ever begin to imagine. Ask God, like Rahab, to save you from death. Because of the One Who has come to us from the lineage of Rahab, because of Jesus Christ, God will give you life."

This sermon from Azurdia says it so clearly. We are all bad people. God gets nothing good when He saves us. For example, look at the Ten Commandments (Exodus 20:1-17): have you ever put anything more important than God? Have you ever made a God to suit yourself – created an image of a god in your mind that doesn't match that God of the Bible? Have you ever taken the name of the Lord in vain? Used His name casually or in an irreverent way (using His name instead of a cuss word when expressing disgust or surprise)? Have you always kept the Sabbath Day every single Sunday of your life? Have you <u>always</u> honored your mom and dad every day of your life? Ever murdered anyone (God sees hatred as murder – Matt. 5:21-22)? Ever committed adultery (God sees lust as adultery – Matt. 5:27-28)? Ever stolen anything, regardless of the value? Ever told a lie, even a "little white" one? Ever wished your had something that someone else has (coveting) instead of being thankful for the blessings that God has already provided? We are all guilty of breaking at least one of these commandments. We bring Him nothing, not even our "good" works can be called good. Scripture says all our good works are like filthy rags (Isaiah 64:6). Because of what Christ did on the cross by paying the penalty of our sin on His behalf, God now sees us as righteous after we repent of (turn from) our sins and put our complete trust in Jesus Christ alone. Only by repentance of sins and faith in Jesus Christ alone can our "court case" be legally dismissed. Our account gets credited with Christ's blood payment and we are then seen as righteous in God's eyes.

We can then face God on Judgment Day, our day in court with Almighty God, with a completely clean slate knowing for sure that our eternity will be spent with our Savior. Can you think of anything better than that? It's the kindest thing a person has ever done for another. God demands perfection. It is impossible for humans to meet that standard. So God Himself became a man, Jesus Christ, while remaining 100% God, and lived a perfect life. Then He died on the cross taking the punishment that we rightfully deserve. God then raised Him from the dead in order to defeat death. He did all this so that we could have His perfection applied to us through repentance and faith in Him, which is the only key to eternal life in Heaven.

People think, and are often told from the pulpit, that they have to do something to get to heaven or that they must contribute to their salvation in some way. This is a complete lie, and one that has its origins in the Catholic church. This is at the heart of false conversion and this is what Lori got tripped up on all the time. I thought that my good works were going to outweigh the bad stuff I was doing and therefore grant me entrance into Heaven. I had to realize there was nothing apart from Christ that I could do to save myself. Nothing. Vince just thought he was saved because he had said a prayer at an altar at a church when he was five years old – and doesn't even remember what he said in that prayer! In Vince's words, "I do, however, as I said in chapter 1, know that the prayer I prayed, whatever it was, did not save me. If it had, I would have continued to live a life of fruitfulness, and obedience to God's Word." Again, we are not saying we will reach perfection in this life.

As Christians we still sin, but we will begin to sin less and less the more we obey God's Word by the power of the Holy Spirit (John 14:16). Repentance involves a deliberate change of direction. You were going one way, now you decide do a 180 and go completely different direction. Don Green says it this way, "Jesus' call to repentance requires the sinner to transfer his entire heart allegiance to Christ . . . You cannot repent and keep any of the desires of your unregenerate heart."

In Matthew 10:37, Jesus says that if you love your father, mother, son, or daughter more than Him is not worthy of Him.

Don goes on to say, "It must be settled that there is nothing on earth that approaches your love for Christ – there is nothing that competes with the final affections of your heart. If it's a matter of choosing between Christ and life you gladly bear the wounds of a martyr. If it's a matter of a family relationship competing with your love for Christ, while we don't seek nor turn people away from us in our human love, if they come and say, 'It's me or Christ', you get up and say,' Here, let me get the door for you as my final act of kindness to you, because I will not turn from Christ.' Jesus doesn't take second place. You give him first place, or you walk away from Him, but don't insult the Son of God with the sense that you'll add Him to your other desires and He'll get fit in the mix someplace. Christ gets the preeminent affection, or you don't get Christ. Everything that you loved before is now subordinated to Christ." (15)

Following Christ means your life, as you know it is over and you give Christ absolute authority to run your life. It's not about you anymore. You are finished. Christ is now your Master, and you are His grateful slave because of what He did for you in His death and resurrection. There is no alternative. Friends, you will search the Scriptures in vain to find a verse or passage about a "sinner's prayer", "accept Christ", or "Ask Jesus into your heart." The Bible simply does not say that's how to be saved. Simply believing in Jesus does not save someone. It's turning from sins and putting your complete trust in the finished work of Christ for salvation that saves you. The sinner needs to realize that he must beg Christ to accept Him! We don't need to approve Him; we need Him to approve us! Repentance from sins and faith in Jesus Christ alone is THE only way to salvation. There is no other way.

Acts 4:12 says, "And there is salvation in no one else; for there is no other name under heaven that has been given among men by which we must be saved." John 14:6 says, "Jesus said to him,'I am THE way, and the truth, and the life; no one comes to the Father BUT through Me." (emphasis ours)

Chapter 10

A Call to Men

"No soldier in active service entangles himself in the affairs of everyday life, so that he may please the one who enlisted him as a soldier. Also if anyone competes as an athlete, he does not win the prize unless he competes according to the rules." 2 Timothy 2:4-5

"When I was a child, I used to speak like a child, think like a child, reason like a child; when I became a man, I did away with childish things." I Corinthians 13:11

Men, this chapter is solely for us. Before I begin, however, I must point out the fact that if you are not a born-again Christian who's heart has not been transformed by the Holy Spirit, please don't read any further. If you are *not sure* you are born again according to the Scriptures and think that you might be a victim of false conversion, please stop reading now. If you are in either of those categories, stop now and examine yourself to see if you are in the faith. Nothing in this chapter really matters unless the source- your heart – is right before God.

2 Corinthians 13:5 says,
"Test yourselves to see if your in the faith: Examine yourselves! Or do you not recognize this about yourselves, that Jesus Christ is in you – unless you fail the test?"

Falsified

    Paul's point is to say that if the Holy Spirit resides in us, then our desires will be to obey what He commands, but if our hearts are not regenerated by the Holy Spirit, our desires will be to continue in our sins by disregarding the commandments of God. So please consider this before continuing to read.

    Now with that being said, let me ask a question: What is a man? I used to be a horrible, wretched man. I still am a horrible, wretched man, but the Holy Spirit has given me a new heart, and He, through God's Word, is leading my heart in a new direction. There are so many books on the market today that talk about being a man, or about what it means to be a real man. I remember, a long time ago, reading John Eldridge's book Wild at Heart. I was probably in my 20's at the time living my "good, moral life" that is taught in most modern-day seeker-driven "Christian" churches. I always wanted to improve my life just like everyone else, so that book really captured my attention. It didn't take me very long to read it. In fact, I sped through it — couldn't put it down. It really did change my life for a while, morally. It challenged me to be a man's man by saying something along the lines of "You're a real man when you go gun down a wild boar, or camp out in the woods for a week alone while living off berries and squirrels." It told me that man needs, wants, and should do these things, and should endeavor to find God in those things, or in doing those things. Wild at Heart even appealed to me (and many other men who read it) by relating most of its so-called "principles" to famous and classic movies in which the lead man did spectacular things, or captured a city, etc. The point was that God supposedly has put these desires into the heart of every man, and man should follow that supposed God-given desire. I had, indeed, seen most of the movies mentioned in the book: those gory, blasphemous, violent, sexualized movies. I wanted to be the hero man in those movies! I didn't see it then, but I see it clearly now, now that I have a new heart operated by the Holy Spirit. I see that the only principles I need for life and Godliness are found in God's Word. Not movies. Hollywood obviously doesn't live for God, so why should we look to their sources for principles to live a Godly life?

Men, we don't need movies to tell us how to be a man of God. Most movies portray men as liars, thieves, blasphemers, adulterers, fornicators, murderers, and coveters.

On the other hand, Scripture has much to say about men, about our speech and our actions. We'll cover a few things about being a man, but first we'll cover husbands specifically. I will also add this: before God saved me, I endeavored to do none of what I'm about to say in this chapter. It was actually impossible because I didn't have the Holy Spirit residing in me to empower me. I still mess up big time, but there has been a significant difference in my marriage since God saved me and now have the power of the Holy Spirit in me. I love being married. God has given me an amazing, Godly wife who helps me learn things about myself I might have never known before. It's been a fun, sanctifying, and hopefully God glorifying experience.

Scripture tells men to be the spiritual leaders of their homes.

> *Ephesians 5:1 says, "Therefore, be imitators of God, as beloved children;" and then later on in verses 25-30, "Husbands, love your wives, just at Christ also loved the church, and gave Himself up for her, so that He might sanctify her, having cleansed her by the washing of water with the Word, that He might present to Himself the church in all her glory, having no spot or wrinkle or any such thing; but that she would be holy and blameless. So husbands ought to love their own wives as their own bodies. He who loves his own wife loves himself;* <u>for no one ever hated his own flesh, but nourishes and cherishes it, just as Christ also does the church.</u>*" (emphasis added)*

Here we see that husbands should treat our wives not only as good as we treat ourselves, but we should be willing to give our very lives for her. That should be a daily endeavor, to give up your rights, as Christ did to serve and show love for your wife. She should do the same, but she should be able to follow our example of service as the leader of the home. Being imitators of God logically means doing what His Word says to do, through the power of the Holy Spirit at work in us. It also means we need

Falsified

to live out the Gospel in our homes every day. We also need to preach the Gospel to ourselves every day – reminding ourselves that we are the worst person in our home - the worst sinner – and God still loves us even though we continually mistreat Him. When we begin to view ourselves as the worst sinner in our homes when it comes to loving our wives, it should, over time, eliminate most arguments and such things. The reason it should do that it because we will have been leading the way through repentance, toward God first, then our wives.

Now let's get to men in general.

> *Matthew 16:24 says,*
> *"Then Jesus said to His disciples, 'If anyone wishes to come after Me, he must deny himself, and take up his cross and follow Me.'"*

Denying ourselves is not easy, but we must be endeavoring to do it daily. We must choose to walk daily in God's Truth.

> *Psalm 119:1-2 says,*
> *"How blessed are those whose way is blameless, who walk in the Law of the Lord. How blessed are those who observe His testimonies, who seek Him with all their heart."*

Walking daily in His Truth transforms our hearts more and more over time.

Proverbs 23:7a says,

> *"For as he thinks within himself, so he is."*

Men, Scripture says that our hearts are deceitful above ALL things, and desperately wicked (Jeremiah 17:9). This, of course, applies to men and women, but we're talking about men right now. We cannot trust our hearts, but we can lead our hearts only by the power of the Holy Spirit, and only using the instructions found in God's Word. There is nothing in this world more powerful and sufficient than God's Word by which we can lead our hearts into God's truth and into obedience to Him.

Men also tend to have a big problem with speech and joking. Most men, even Christian men that I've been around, will laugh and joke about crude things. I'm not going to go into detail about this, because I'm pretty sure you know what I am talking about.

> Ephesians 5:3-4 says,
> "But immorality or any impurity or greed must not even be named among you, as is proper among saints; and there must be no filthiness and silly talk, or coarse jesting, which are not fitting, but rather giving of thanks."

This is another way that men should lead the way into Godliness. These verses clearly say that any impurity must not be named because saints (born-again Christians) should be acting differently than the world. Silly talk and coarse jesting are not fitting among saints. Paul is telling Christians that foolish talking and crude jokes should not be part of our speech/conversations. What do you joke about around the dinner table? What jokes do you laugh at when you are around your co-workers and friends? Is there a difference between you and your unsaved friends?

In Ephesians 4:1, Paul tells Christians,

> "Therefore, I, the prisoner of the Lord, implore you to walk in a manner worthy of the calling with which you have been called."

If we are Christians, we should be acting like it! Paul IMPLORES us to do so. We must be different from the world in our speech and actions. Paul tells us to conduct ourselves in such a way that is worthy of the gospel of Christ (Philippians 1:27a), and to set our minds on things above, not on earthly things (Colossians 3:2).

I heard a fantastic Sunday school lesson when visiting Grace Community Church in which Tom Patton (one of the elders) spoke about Proverbs in reference to lazy men. Much of Proverbs is Solomon giving Godly instructions to his son.

> *Proverbs 6:9-15 says,*
>
> *"How long will you lie down, O sluggard? When will you arise from your sleep? A little sleep, a little slumber, A little folding of the hands to rest"— Your poverty will come in like a vagabond And your need like an armed man. A worthless person, a wicked man, Is the one who walks with a perverse mouth, who winks with his eyes, who signals with his feet, who points with his fingers; who with perversity in his heart continually devises evil, who spreads strife. Therefore his calamity will come suddenly; instantly he will be broken and there will be no healing."*

Clearly Solomon has nothing good to say about a lazy man, or lazy people in general. Being the leaders in our homes, again, this is a huge area that affects much, if not the majority, of "Christian" men in today's culture. Lazy men aren't really men at all, but rather boys in a man's body. The current trend for men is to go to work, hopefully not work too hard, come home, and sit in front of the TV all evening, or play the latest and "coolest" video game for hours. That is plain lazy. It is also a waste of time. I'll mention social media very briefly here because it can be a very dangerous or very useful tool. Lori and I don't use Facebook or MySpace or any other "social networking/media" sites such as those because of several reasons, some of which Lori mentions in her chapter for women later on, but right now I'll mention one big reason. Some may call some of what I'm saying "legalism", but legalism by definition is earning your way to Heaven. What I'm talking about is Christianity. It's Biblical discretion and discernment for the glory of God. If you are a man who uses one of these "social media" sites, ask yourself this question, which we've asked many people who have these type of accounts: If you are not preaching the Gospel, or exalting the name of Christ in ALL your social media endeavors, then what is the point? Seriously.

Paul Washer says it well, speaking especially to men, "*I'll tell you this right now, some of you need to get out of Facebook, you need to get offline, you need to quit playing with people and talking and writing little things like you were a little girl. You need to become a man, and start doing things that men of God do.*" (http://vimeo.com/3536737)

Scripture instructs us in many places about using our time, but in Ephesians 5:15-16, Paul instructs us to

> *"Therefore be careful how you walk, not as unwise men but as wise, making the most of your time, because the days are evil."*

We should 1) be careful, 2) walk as wise men, and 3) make wise use of our time. We should be being leaders in these areas not only as an example of Godliness for the world to see, but for eternal purposes, and ultimately for the glory of our Savior.

Titus 2:6-8 gives instructions to young men, which logically should be followed by all other men in general – in all things to be an example of good deeds, "purity in doctrine, dignified, sound in speech which is beyond reproach" so that someone watching you live your life will be shamed, "having NOTHING bad to say about us." (emphasis mine) Men, we have a very high calling from our Savior and King. It's hard sometimes, but very attainable by the power of the Holy Spirit if you're born-again. If you have been trying to do these things, and the things I'll mention later, and it just doesn't seem to ever happen and things are not changing, it is a good sign that you are a false convert. Again, none of this can effectively take place long term without the Holy Spirit residing in you to empower you along the way.

There are three more brief things that I am going to mention before closing this chapter. Everyone's biggest sin is idolatry. Idolatry is the root of every sin. Every man's (and every woman's) heart is prone to worship everything else but God. Anything in our lives that we are consistently making more important than God, or equally as important as God, is an idol. What's yours? Sports? Video games? Television? Pornography? God hates idolatry (Exodus 20:3). As leaders in our home, our primary focus should be, as the Psalmist says,

> *"Open my eyes, that I may behold Wonderful things from Your law."*
> *"I have restrained my feet from every evil way, that I may keep Your word."*

> *"I have inherited Your testimonies forever, For they are the joy of my heart. I have inclined my heart to perform Your statutes Forever, even to the end."* Psalm 119:18,101,111,112.

All Godly men should strive to attain to the characteristics from 1 Timothy 3:1-10 – be above reproach, temperate, prudent, hospitable, not addicted to much wine, not pugnacious, free from the love of money – for the glory of God.

Physical appearance is an idol for many Christian men, and why not? The world bombards us with images of "buff" or "hunky" men. Notice two key words there – the world. Many men are plagued with the false idea that physical appearance is what makes a man. I am not saying that there is anything wrong with bodily exercise, but it should be very low on our priority list.

> I Samuel 16:7 says,
> *"But the Lord said to Samuel, 'Do not look at his appearance or at the height of his stature, because I have rejected him; for God sees not as man sees, for man looks at the outward appearance, but the Lord looks at the heart."*

Of course this passage does not apply directly to us, nor it is speaking directly about how we should or should not look, but a principle to take from this is that the Lord sees the heart, not the outward appearance.

> 1 Timothy 4:8 says,
> *"for bodily discipline is only of little profit, but Godliness if profitable for all things, since it holds promise for the present life and also for the life to come."*

Finally and very briefly, pornography. Men, if you are into pornography in any way, shape or form, stop. Quit it. Kill it! You can do it only by the power of the Holy Spirit, praise be to His name, but you can do it. You must do it!

Every time you look at those filthy images, you are committing adultery against your wife, or if you are single, against God. Every time you poison your soul with pornography, you are telling your Covenant Partner and Savior that you are siding with His enemy. You are hurting yourself, your wife, your family, and most importantly you are killing your soul. Do whatever it takes to kill pornography. Jesus Christ died for you and you are willing to continually slap your Savior in the face with this evil sin? Kill it. Now. Your Savior is ready for your repentance.

(Visit wretchedradio.com for Todd Friel's Slaying the Dragon).

Men, what is really important to you, what really is important to you? Seriously. Is there any other thing that you think you must have in life besides Christ and His Word? I will end with two things. I have woven together some quotes from Dr. John MacArthur, and song lyrics from Christian singer Steve Green.

First, the lyrics from Steve Green's "Oh Men of God, Arise":

> Oh men of God arise, awake from slumber's night, shake off sin's drowsiness and rouse yourself to fight.
> Run from vain distractions, keep your vision clear; cast out all fleshly stowaways, refuse to harbor fear.
> Lift up the cup of holiness, drink long and take your fill, oh men of God arise to carry out, to carry out God's will.
> Oh men of God arise, take up your sword and shield. Your foe has no defense against the power they wield.
> Christ has gained the victory the outcome is assured, Satan is defeated by the power of God's word.
> Lift up the cup of holiness, drink long and take your fill, oh men of God arise to carry out, to carry out God's will.
> Oh men of God arise, and face the eastern skies, for Christ will soon descend with lightning in his eyes.
> Then our ancient foe long vanquished will meet his rightful end, and sin's dark night of terror will never fall again.

> Lift up the cup of holiness, drink long and take your fill.
> Oh men of God arise to carry out, to carry out God's will.

Finally, a fitting end, Dr. MacArthur says,

"We as men of God today take our place in the ranks of those who are the historic spokesmen for the eternal God. In 2 Timothy 2:17, Paul refers to THE man of God, referring not just to Timothy, but to all who fall into that category. All Scripture is inspired by God, profitable for teaching, reproof, correction, training in righteousness, that THE man of God may be adequate, equipped for every good work. He is known by what he flees from. In 1 Corinthians 6:18 the Apostle Paul says, 'Flee sexual sin', 10:14 says 'Flee idolatry', 2 Timothy 2:22 Paul writes to Timothy 'Flee youthful lusts'. We are fleeing. The man of God is fleeing at all times those kinds of corrupting things. How can you speak for God unless you know the message of God? You cannot know the message of God apart from Scripture. All Scripture then is given to us as men of God that we may be perfected or made adequate to the proclamation of the Word of God which is what it means to be a man of God."(14)

Chapter 11

A Call to Women

An excellent wife, who can find? For her worth is far above jewels. The heart of her husband trusts in her. And he will have no lack of gain. Proverbs 31:10-11

Charm is deceitful and beauty is vain, But a woman who fears the Lord, she shall be praised. Proverbs 31:30

"Older women likewise are to be reverent in their behavior, not malicious gossips not enslaved to much wine, teaching what is good, so that they may encourage young women to love their husbands, to love their children, to be sensible, pure, workers at home, kind, being subject to their own husbands, so that the word of God will not be dishonored." Titus 2:3-5

Drawing attention to myself was something I did before I was saved. It was all about me, my looks, my personality, and how much fun I could have. Everything that the Proverbs teach about in a godly woman was far from my concept of view. God has a calling for men, but He also has a high calling for women in that supportive role and in how they are to esteem the Lord above all else. Many times those things get skewed and out of view when you are lost. They get even blurrier when you are a false convert.

The reason being is that you tend to justify out your actions because you are a "good girl" and you are saved, so you are okay. That is exactly what I did in my early twenties. I tried to weigh the scales with my immodest dress and behavior by going to church on Sunday and saying that I was doing the right thing in God's eyes. I was making my own God into the image I wanted Him to be, not as His holy and just nature of who He truly is. When you are walking in the biblical principles of a godly woman that is saved and lives for the Lord your life alters in every way.

As a single woman, your view of how to go about dating and allowing the Lord to choose your husband is guided by His word, not your heart. Because the scripture clearly says in Jeremiah 17:9,

"The heart is deceitful than all else, And is desperately sick."

When I was single and totally lost, I let my heart and emotions control my thought life. What a disaster that was. You may be able to identify with this idea if you are lost and allowing yourself to ride the emotional roller coaster of dating guy after guy. You are not grounded in the Lord's truths and equipping yourself with the word to guide you in those decisions. Obviously in a perfect world our father's should be guarding our hearts and helping us in that important decision of dating and marriage. But there are many out there that don't have that relationship with their father where he will step in and protect that area for a girl. If you have one of those dad's appreciate him and trust that he has your best interest at heart and that the Lord is working in his life to care for you in that way. However if you don't have that guidance in your life in a physical sense above all else, we as women should be looking to the Lord for our wisdom and direction, even if we have a good father figure.

As the Psalmist says in Chapter 91 verse 2,

*"I will say to the
Lord, "My refuge and my fortress, My God, in whom I trust!"*

We need to remember this in all things that we are to cling to Him as our refuge. Not put our security in men, shopping, pampering ourselves, friendships, our work, or whatever else we cling to that helps fill up the void. The end result is always insecurity. If your hope or your sense of identity comes in the form of anything other than your relationship with God, you have a priority problem. How do we get that right? How do we keep the Lord first and foremost of our lives? Constant study of His word and mediating on what it says to do. Focusing on His principles for living a disciplined life and a character that reflects His nature. Ladies, do we think that idle chatter and gossip reflect the character of our Lord. Absolutely not! Why do we search for who we are in the value of another's eyes?

> *I will give thanks to You, for I am fearfully and wonderfully made; Wonderful are Your works, And my soul knows it very well. Psalm 139:14*

Read that passage again . . . for I am fearfully and wonderfully made. Wonderful are YOUR works, and MY soul knows it very well. Friend, if we read the words given from our Lord Jesus, why don't we let those give way to our attention and focus. Who cares what you wear to work, church, or school. Who cares what someone said about you. When you realize that the Lord of all creation has made you and done so wonderfully, why do you need the approval of man or in many cases, women. I guess that's the point I want to get across very clearly in this chapter because for far too long I lived a life of nothing but self absorbed me and gossip and immodesty. There are other issues that come with being a biblical woman, but if we first aren't saved that is the root issue. After we are saved we should be doing everything with the help of the Holy Spirit in us to conform to the image of Christ. You have to get that principle and concept down before you can even address the secondary issues that come with developing into a biblical woman. So, dear friend if you are reading this and you think you are saved but you look at your life and it looks no different from the unsaved girl next to you, it might be time for self-examination.

A woman that fears the Lord as mentioned in the verse at the first of this chapter wants nothing to come between her and her relationship with Christ. This means if you are living with your boyfriend, but call yourself a Christian, these two things don't line up with scripture. This means if you are going out on the weekends and partying and dressing in ways that invite unwelcome attention, this does not glorify the King of Kings. This means if you are engaging in office gossip or social media idle chatter of nothing but worldly things, this time killer is not pleasing to the Lord of Hosts. You can't have the Holy Spirit living in you and living a life of contradiction. The conviction should and will eat you up inside. He wants us to live our lives that are a reflection of who is in charge of your life, those things I just listed are a reflection of self . . . not Jesus Christ.

In mention of the topic of gossip, and ladies, we can find ourselves easily entrapped into that concept, you have to set boundaries for yourself. If a conversation starts going that direction, you have to bow out. I've had the chance to do it gracefully and other times I've had to just be bold and take a stance. Its not always easy, but I don't want to be a stumbling block to another.

> *"Woe to the world because of its stumbling blocks! For it is inevitable that stumbling blocks come; but woe to that man through whom the stumbling block comes!" Matthew 18:7*

That's a pretty heavy verse. We are warned not to lead anyone astray by our actions and cause a stumbling block to them. That can go for a multitude of areas that we women engage in. As I stated earlier, if your social media site is causing you to get trapped up into the area of gossip and idle chatter, delete it. Vince and I don't have any type of social media site for the sake of just removing any additional stumbling blocks in our marriage. Its been said that 50% of divorce cases nowadays are directly related to facebook and other social media sites. Christian marriages have a big enough target on their backs, that we did not think we needed to add all the dangers that arise from those sites and would encourage you to consider the same option.

I just think you have to error on the side of caution when it comes to conforming to being a godly woman. This also includes how you dress. I used to think the trendier and glitterier, the better. I had no idea just how much attention I was drawing to myself until after I got saved. I walked into that closet and began to realize not only was I not dressing my age, but also I was dressing immodestly and childish to be honest. A mature Christian woman who is growing in godliness and holiness wants the attention to be on Christ, not on her. I am not opposed to women wearing pants or anything like that, but you might just take stock in what you have in your wardrobe and if its tight, low, sheer, or short . . . get rid of it. The power we as women have on men and the visual-ness they see is incredible. They struggle daily with lust, why would you entice that as a godly woman? Lust is a huge issue that leads into pornography and other addictions; you don't want to be a party to that. I know women say, I can dress how I want, I'm not responsible for what that man does. That is not only irresponsible but also very selfish. We should all be helping one another to finish out the race strong. You don't want to cause your Christian brother to stumble, or an unbeliever by what they see on you rather than in you. Again, if you are single, that is not the type of guy you want to attract. You want someone who sees the motive and content of your heart and wants to pursue that, not your body. If you are married, ask your husband before you go out if your outfit is inappropriate. As I was going through this process of cleaning out my closet, I would have to do that on occasion because my brain was still so conditioned to what the world wears and views as attractive, that I needed help in that refining process. I've since gotten pretty good at not even needing to ask Vince about the attire, I decided if I have to question it, then I better get rid of it.

Now if you are like me, this eliminated a lot of your wardrobe. I have a solution. I prayed and told the Lord I wanted to conform more to His image in this area and really start dressing more modest and less attention grabbing. I found out about consignment stores. I took all of my clothes up to the consignment store (if the clothes were really bad, I threw them completely away because I didn't want to encourage that in other women) but for the items that basically looked like a teenybopper and were salvageable in that way, I sold them to consignment. The money I got back I would then go and little by little rebuild my wardrobe to things I could be comfortable in. The other thing I did was widdle down the amount of my clothes . . . a lot. When I was single and lost, shopping had been an outlet of fun and more indulgence of self, so I had a lot of clothes. You don't need a lot of clothes. That was another key to this area of understanding. Less was definitely more in this department. I found a nice thrift store by the house and they have basically brand new items and name brand items, not that it matters at all, but for under 5 bucks! These are just some tips at helping you to overcome this area in your life. It can be a hard one for women, but it shouldn't be when we are trying to exemplify Christ in EVERY area of our lives.

I want to interject at this point with some very wise advice from Dr John MacArthur on some of these topics mentioned above that he did in a sermon series entitled God's High Calling for Women and this coming from the fourth in that series, "1 Timothy 2, beginning at verse 9:

"In like manner also, that women adorn themselves in proper apparel, with godly fear and self-control. Not with braided hair, gold or pearls or expensive clothing. But which is fitting women professing godliness with good works. Let the women learn, in silence with all subjection. But I permit the not a woman to teach, nor to usurp authority over the man, but to be in silence. For Adam was first formed, then Eve. And Adam was not deceived but the woman being deceived was in the transgression. Nevertheless, she shall be saved in childbearing, if they continue in faith and love and holiness with self control." So, from verse 9 through 15, Paul gives us six elements of this very important instruction regarding the role of women in the church.

Now, you'll remember that the first thing he speaks about is their appearance.

How are women to appear in the church? You remember verse 9 says, "that women are to adorn themselves in a proper adorning." In other words, they are to appear in a way that expresses love for God, reverence for His holiness, an attitude of worship. The latter part of the verse indicates that they are not to occupy themselves with outward fashion, they are not to flaunt their wealth, and he refers in the plaiting of the hair and gold and pearls, to a common custom where, since women were so fully clad in that culture from neck to . . . to the ground, the way they would flaunt their wealth was in their hair. And they would weave gold and pearls and tortoise shell combs would be placed into their hair and this way could, they could show their wealth. They could flaunt themselves. That was the way women adorned themselves in a carnal expression in that time. And what he is saying here is that should not happened in the church. The tendency of women to be preoccupied with their adornment is only a manifestation of the carnality of their hearts. Dressing to flaunt wealth, dressing to, a, manifest lust and sexual desire. Dressing to express a spirit of insubordination to one's husband. These are forbidden a woman who appears to worship God.

Secondly, he discussed their attitude.

In the middle of verse 9, their attitude is to be one of godly fear and self control. Godly fear comes from a root word, meaning they have a sense of shame. In other words, they are to be ashamed of causing anyone to be distracted from the worship and the glory of God. They have a proper sense of shame that results in modesty. And self-control refers to being able to control your passion and your desire. Women are to present themselves then, in modesty and humbleness of heart, demonstrating total control over their passion and appearing in such a way as draws attention to their godliness and their virtue.

Thirdly, in verse 10, we discuss their testimony.

If they make profession of godliness, they should support that with good works. So you have not only their appearance and their

Falsified

attitude, but their activity, or their action. Their deeds should also demonstrate that profession of godliness which they bear.

This is amazingly good advice and biblical mandates for women in how they are to live according to scripture as a professing Christian. Remember these areas and practice self control when you come to these topics of modesty, speech, motive, and your place in your home and the church.

Perfectionism is another trap ladies fall into. We have to keep up with so and so just to have a clean house, a meal on the table at 5, perfect skin, a nice yard or whatever it may be. The only perfect person was Jesus Christ. We will never live up to that. Just accept it and quit beating yourself up for not being numero uno at every thing you tackle. Paul tells us to be content in all things.

> *Phillipians 4:12 states" I know how to get along with humble means, and I also know how to live in prosperity; in any and every circumstance I have learned the secret of being filled and going hungry, both of having abundance and suffering need." We need to be putting that into practice.*

This is an area I still submit to the Lord all the time. I have a tendency to want to control things and this is a sin. We are to trust the Lord, not worry, and to commit all of our ways to Him.

> *Matthew 6:34 reminds us ""So do not worry about tomorrow; for tomorrow will care for itself. Each day has enough trouble of its own."*

Conforming to His likeness in this way is so freeing and it allows you to walk in obedience to the Lord rather than being the Lord of your own life. Self-confidence, worry, and guilt are all common themes that you hear worldly women and even professing Christian women admit to. It just seems to be the normal thing now to be stressed out, over worked, and having too many irons in the fire. It has gotten to the point that if you don't have a job, kids, a husband, going to the gym, hosting parties, and making a meal for every need of someone in the church you just aren't good enough. That is the world's standard of a woman's role. That is not God's standard. Root yourself in His word and trust that He is enough to provide for all your needs, that you don't have to do it all, have it all, be it all to everyone. Release yourself from that bondage of being the perfect worldly woman and focus on being more like the Proverbs 31 woman and serving God, honoring your husband if your are married, taking care of your children, and then helping others.

I want to say a word to wives for a minute. Being married over 3 years now I guess I am technically still a newlywed, I'm not sure when that term dissipates, but the greatest calling I have in life is being a wife and my biggest ministry is to Vince, (Genesis 2:18) I love it more than anything and consider it all as joy. It has been the best source of refining who I am to be more like Christ than anything I've ever experienced. The Lord gave me something far greater in my husband than just a provider and mate; He gave me a best friend who literally is my sharpening iron. He helps to guide me when I am falling into sin with either a negative attitude or a wrong motive. The Lord has allowed my husband to be that person that truly leads our home.

The topic of submission is so taboo nowadays with all the women's liberation movements and this dominance of women everywhere it seems. When submission is practiced rightly, it is the most beautiful and biggest release you can experience as a wife.

> *"Wives be subject to your own husbands, as to the Lord. For the husband is the head of the wife, as Christ also is the head of the church, He Himself being the Savior of the body. But as the church is subject to Christ, so also the wives ought to be to their husbands in everything." Ephesians 5:22-24*

The marriage relationship is a direct picture of Christ and the church. It does not matter if your husband is not saved, it does not matter if he doesn't give you the attention you think you deserve, it does not matter if he is a hypocrite. You are commanded to love and submit to him. You are to do this to the Lord and therefore in obedience to Him, you do this for your husband. He has his own commands he is to follow, but regardless of if he is doing those or not, it does not negate your role as a wife to submit to his authority and leadership. Obviously there is clear command that if he asks of anything that is in violation to scripture you are not commanded to obey that, but apart from that, he is your husband and you are called to be an example of the church lovingly being obedient to the Savior. When this is done harmoniously in marriage, it can be a truly safe and loving environment. When any part of the love, respect, submission and authority gets skewed, the entire thing derails. You keep doing your part and what the Lord has commanded of you and the Lord will deal with the other party. We as biblical women are called to support our husbands, to love them, to give them the respect they deserve as the head of the household. I can't say it enough, don't nag your husband. It does nothing but tear him down on the inside and out. Give him over to the Lord continually in prayer. He needs those prayers. Men have a very high calling from the Lord and the world, they need their wives support.

Trust me, two falsely saved people living under one roof after saying "I do" was quite a challenge. As I said before when I first met Vince, I did know that he was to be my husband. I didn't know that the Lord would radically save us from hell, sin, judgment and His wrath and ultimately ourselves. It was the greatest thing that could ever happen to not only myself, but to our marriage. Being a false convert and entering into marriage is very dangerous. You think you are saved and therefore shouldn't be treating this person this way, but somehow you are. I thank God when I look back and realize that was my flesh treating Vince that way, because I know now that had I been saved, there is no way I could of acted that way. Once the Holy Spirit came in, He tamed my tongue, my strong will, my controlling nature, and above all else, my selfishness.

Precious friend, if you are reading this and haven't been living a life that reflects a godly woman, I pray that you would start to dive into the Word and meditate on it. Obviously we are not going to be complete Proverbs 31 women overnight, but we can start to move in that direction and allow the Lord to shape our lives into that over time. Remember, let the things you do, say, wear, reflect, watch, and listen to, all be a portrait of exemplifying the character of a woman who says, I love Jesus Christ above all else.

Epilogue

The topic of forgiveness is definitely something that we wanted to address in this book and there was a story that I (Lori) had heard about and was quickly overwhelmed by it. I then shared it with Vince and he too was overcome by the power of God's forgiveness in it.

Many have heard of "The Son of Sam" story that occurred back in the late seventies. David Berkowitz was that man. His story of conversion is what that moved us from shock to surprise to tears. His testimony is one of true redemption and forgiveness. We'll let his own words share this with you (these passages were taken from his full testimony (16):

"Ever since I was a small child, my life seemed to be filled with torment. I would often have seizures in which I would roll on the floor. Sometimes furniture would get knocked over. When these attacks came, it felt as if something was entering me. During this period of my life I was also plagued with bouts of severe depression. When this feeling came over me, I would hide under my bed for hours. I would also lock myself in a closet and sit in total darkness from morning until afternoon. I had a craving for the darkness and I felt an urge to flee away from people. Thoughts of suicide often came into my mind. Sometimes I spent time sitting on a window ledge with my legs dangling over the side.

We lived on the 6th floor of an old apartment building. When my dad saw me doing this he would yell at me to get back inside.

I also felt powerful urges to step in front of moving cars or throw myself in front of subway trains. At times those urges were so strong that my body actually trembled. I remember that it was a tremendous struggle for me to hold on to my sanity.

I had no idea what to do and neither did my parents. They had me talk to a rabbi, teachers and school counselors, but nothing worked. In 1975, however, I met some guys at a party who were, I later found out, heavily involved in the occult. I had always been fascinated with witchcraft, satanism, and occult things since I was a child. When I was growing up I watched countless horror and satanic movies, one of which was Rosemary's Baby. That movie in particular totally captivated my mind.

Now I was age 22 and this evil force was still reaching out to me. Everywhere I went there seemed to be a sign or a symbol pointing me to Satan. I felt as if something were trying to take control of my life. I began to read the Satanic Bible by the late Anton LaVey who founded the Church of Satan in San Francisco in 1966. I began, innocently, to practice various occult rituals and incantations.

I am utterly convinced that something satanic had entered into my mind and that, looking back at all that happened, I realize that I had been slowly deceived. I did not know that bad things were going to result from all this. Yet over the months the things that were wicked no longer seemed to be such. I was headed down the road to destruction and I did not know it. Maybe I was at a point where I just didn't care anymore. Eventually I crossed that invisible line of no return. After years of mental torment, behavioral problems, deep inner struggles and my own rebellious ways, I became the criminal that, at the time, it seemed as if it was my destiny to become.

Looking back it was all a horrible nightmare and I would do anything if I could undo everything that happened. Six people lost their lives. Many others suffered at my hand, and will continue to suffer for a lifetime. I am so sorry for that.

Falsified

In 1978 I was sentenced to about 365 consecutive years, virtually burying me alive behind prison walls. When I first entered the prison system I was placed in isolation. I was then sent to a psychiatric hospital because I was declared temporarily insane. Eventually I was sent to other prisons including the infamous Attica.

As with many inmates, life in prison is a struggle. I have had my share of problems, hassles and fights. At one time I almost lost my life when another inmate cut my throat. Yet all through this – and I did not realize it until later – God had His loving hands on me. Ten years into my prison sentence and feeling despondent and without hope, another inmate came up to me one day as I was walking the prison yard on a cold winter's night. He introduced himself and began to tell me that Jesus Christ loved me and wanted to forgive me. Although I knew he meant well I mocked him because I did not think that God would ever forgive me or that He would want anything to do with me.

Still this man persisted and we became friends. His name was Rick and we would walk the yard together. Little by little he would share with me about his life and what he believed Jesus had done for him. He kept reminding me that no matter what a person did, Christ stood ready to forgive if that individual would be willing to turn from the bad things they were doing and would put their full faith and trust in Jesus Christ and what He did on the cross by dying for our sins.

He gave me a Gideon's Pocket Testament and asked me to read the Psalms. I did. Every night I would read from them. And it was at this time that the Lord was quietly melting my stone cold heart.

One night, I was reading Psalm 34. I came upon the 6th verse, which says, "this poor man cried, and the Lord heard him, and saved him from all his troubles".

It was at that moment, in 1987, that I began to pour out my heart to God. Everything seemed to hit me at once. The guilt from what I did . . . the disgust at what I had become . . . late that night in my cold cell, I got down on my knees and I began to cry out to Jesus Christ.

I told Him that I was sick and tired of doing evil. I asked Jesus to forgive me for all my sins. I spent a good while on my knees praying to Him. When I got up it felt as if a very heavy but invisible chain that had been around me for so many years was broken. A peace flooded over me. I did not understand what was happening. But in my heart I just knew that my life, somehow, was going to be different.

One of my favorite passages of Scripture is Romans 10:13. It says, "For whosoever shall call upon the name of the Lord shall be saved." Here it is clear that God has no favorites. He rejects no one, but welcomes all who will call upon Him.

I know that God is a God of mercy who is willing to forgive. He is perfectly able to restore and heal our hurting and broken lives. I have discovered from the Bible that Jesus Christ died for our sins. Yet He was without sin. He took our place on that cross. He shed His blood as the full and complete payment God required for our wrongdoing.

The Bible also says, "For all have sinned, and come short of the glory of God (Romans 3:23)." Furthermore, it says, "For the wages of sin is death; but the gift of God is eternal life through Jesus Christ our Lord (Romans 6:23)."

These passages make it clear that everyone has sinned. Yes, some like myself did so more than others. But all have done things wrong. Therefore, we must all make the decision to acknowledge our sins before God and be sorry for them. We need to turn from our lives of sin as well as believe that Christ was and is the Son of God.

You must believe that Jesus Christ died and was buried, and on the third day He rose again in victory, for death could not hold Him. Ask Christ to forgive you. Declare Him as Lord of your life and do not be ashamed to do so. To reject Jesus Christ and His work on the cross is to reject God's perfect and only gift of salvation and eternal life."

If this story of conversion and the power of a forgiving Holy Just God does not just make your heart weep and then celebrate, it should. We as Christians should be celebrating victoriously when any comes to know Christ. All conversion stories are dramatic, the fact that ANY person gets saved and has the hope of heaven as an eternal reward after repentance and trust in Jesus takes place is amazing. Some people want to think that criminals as bad as David Berkowitz should not get heaven, but what they don't realize is that they are no different. In God's eyes we are all the same before we come to Christ. The lies, the blaspheming, the lusting, the stealing-they are all the same as an act of murder in the eyes of a Holy God. They are crimes committed against the Savior. Therefore we are all hell-bound if not for the saving grace of our Lord Jesus Christ. What a loving God that is, that He does not send us all straight to hell, but rather allows for us to be drawn in by the Holy Spirit and have our eyes opened so that we may come to know Him and ask His forgiveness through repenting of our sins. Once we understand this concept of forgiveness, we can then show that same kindness of forgiveness to others. What a good God we serve. What a Just God we honor. What a Holy God that we submit our lives to.

In contrast to David's testimony as you just read, there is another conversion we would like to share with you that is very precious to us. The singer Steve Green as Vince mentioned in the men's chapter has been a huge impact on us not only through his vocal talent, but his testimony hit very close to home. If you think David's story is so far from what you could ever do or be like, listen to the conversion of Steve Green and we pray it will stir you just as it did for us.

According to the episode on the show, "Testimony: Profiles in Faith-Steve Green" we hear a powerful story of false conversion. To paraphrase the episode we have tried to capture the key points for you and some of his direct quotes.

Steve Green grew up in Argentina with parents that were missionaries and actively preaching the gospel. Steve's parents had a deep love for another and that had a great impact on him. He was sent off to boarding school because there was no other option during those years, and he had a similar encounter that we did.

He read a book about missionaries in his room and realized he had never done what they had done so he knelt down by the bed and prayed the prayer in the book. He had an 8 year old's confession of faith moment. He went and told all the kids that he had just became a Christian. At the age of 16 he went back to South America after having been in America and loved it. That was the beginning of his resentment on his return, he desired to be more of an American and his heart moved to the states. Hardness grew and lasted for 10 years he states until he was 26. In his words it was a long dry wandering period. He had come back to the states and was all American. He traveled around with a music group and was big and loud. His family didn't know quite the voice that he had. They knew he could sing good, but not to that level. Steve then got married to Marijean and they started traveling with the Gaithers. A lot happened in the ten years of that dry time period. The stage of what he is doing now was slowing being set. He says he was still in a wasteland spiritually, that he was a Christian externally and went to church but that was about it. I was a "voice for hire. I sang. I was paid to." From outside appearances it looked like a good life and a good marriage. Green states, "There was not the spiritual union" in regard to his marriage. Marijean didn't really have any idea what all was going on with Steve at that time. He says, "If I'm not a captive to Chirst then I'm going to be in some degree or another, a captive to sine to my own passions and desires. And that's where I was." Steve's sister is getting married and his brother Randy picks him up at the airport and Randy had just a revival in his own life. Randy says that God had been burdening his heart to tell what all God had done in him. He was telling Steve and his other brother to get right with God, he was crying and pleading with them. Steve says at this point he is thinking what has happened to this guy, he is weird. For the next three days that's all Randy did was talk about Christ and the change in his life. Steve resented Randy for getting in everyone's face. He was okay with him talking about God, but not all the time, that's not normal. It all finally came to a head in the car when according to Steve, Randy went on another rampage of the topic.

Falsified

"Something inside of me welled up in anger against him. It got to the point where I told him to shut up. Stop. Shut up." At this point, Randy started crying. He knew that the hostility and antagonism in Steve wasn't against him directly, but against the Holy Spirit. He told him, "Steve, you're not resisting me, your resisting the Holy Spirit." In Steve's own words in response, "And you are a liar, what do you know about my life? What right do you have to make any judgement about my life?" Randy then tells him, "I don't know what it is, but there is something wrong with you and I ask that you get it right."

Green says that he ended up on his knees that night and said God I give up. I've been a blatant hypocrite, I've figured out all the church stuff and for ten years I've been doing a tug of war with you and I've been wanting my own way. I don't know you, I don't love you, I don't anything you. And it was at that point Steve got truly saved from his false conversion at eight. He got right with God as Randy pointed out earlier. Steve says he woke up that morning thinking he was top dog and ended up getting smashed. "God smashed me, but it was the best thing in the world. I was an arrogant fool and God changed me."

The first thing that changed after that day was that he had a desire to do right by God. His whole life changed. For two and half weeks he went to people that he had wronged. He paid a lot of restitution and made relationships right that were wronged. He shared with his wife some things that were hard to hear but the Lord allowed forgiveness to take root. She says his whole posture changed from arrogant to humble. Everything started to change. Things just progressed from there. They started traveling together and doing their own ministry and singing and left amicable from the Gaithers. They were singing at churches for a crowd of 35 but they were happy and they were blessed. They did not do any promotions, or cold calls, they just waited to see what the Lord would do and where He would take them. He would share his message with people of where he came from and how the Lord delivered him from bondage. He had a desire to talk and share with people his transformation due to Christ.

Maybe that conversion story hits a little closer to home. It did for us. As we've stated before, just because you grow up in a Christian home and come from that environment, until we are ripped to our core of our own arrogance and pride, can we truly see the need for the Savior in our life. That is exactly what happened to both David Berkowitz and Steve Green and to any truly converted Christian. You are stripped down to nothing but the shell of a person and you see all your sin and your need for the Holy God of this world to save you from yourself, hell and a continual life of spiraling sin. Every conversion is a story of reflection of Christ's atonement. What a beautiful and glorious gift we have been given by Jesus. We hope you stop and think about your eternal state and if it looks anything like the previous lives of ourselves, Steve Green, David Berkowitz, or the world, examine yourself and we urge you to get right with God. Today.

APPENDIX

By Justin Peters

The issue of false conversion is one that is near to my heart; not only because of my interest in proclaiming the truth and combating false doctrine, but also because for many, many years I was a false convert myself. Raised in a Southern Baptist church, I was "saved" and baptized at the age of seven. I knew the proper lingo and prayed the "sinner's prayer." The two elements of genuine conversion are repentance and faith. I had faith in Jesus – just like I had in faith in Santa Clause and the Easter Bunny, for they were real to me as well. That is not biblical faith. As for repentance, well, what is it exactly from which a seven year old can repent? There is no possible way that a child at that age can have any comprehension of the gravity of sin, the holiness of God, His righteousness, wrath, or true repentance and without comprehension of these basics of Christianity, salvation is not possible.

I lived my life as a false convert. I went to seminary as a false convert. I was even preaching and teaching seminars around the world as a false convert. When asked to share my testimony, however, it was always a struggle for me and for good reason – I did not have one. Around 2007 I came across Living Waters

Ministries and Way of the Master (www.livingwaters.com) and learned of the biblical approach to evangelism by the use of Law and grace. It made sense to me and I could see that it was clearly biblical but I had made an intellectual assent only. I even began using this approach in my own evangelism and preaching. Looking back, however, I was using it in a vain attempt to pacify my own guilty conscience. Many were the nights when, after preaching, I would return to my hotel room and lay awake in bed worried that if I were to die in my sleep I would go straight to Hell. God was blessing my ministry to be sure. I received thousands of emails from people all over the world who had been helped by the truth in my seminars. This, however, is why God was blessing my work – because I was preaching and teaching the Truth. God was blessing my work not because of me but *in spite* of me. He was blessing it because of the Truth but the Truth had not yet changed my heart. I used the apparent "success" of my ministry to convince myself of something that was not really true – that I was a Christian. In reality I was living a lie. There was a worldly sorrow over my sin but this only lead to death. I did not have the "godly sorrow (that) worketh repentance to salvation" (2 Cor. 7:10, KJV). I kept trying to repent on my own not realizing that true, effectual repentance does not come this way. True repentance is a gift. It is granted by God Himself (Acts 5:30-31; 11:17, 2 Tim. 2:24-26).

After five months of marriage in January of 2011, God, in His sovereign grace, broke me. He shattered me. For the first time in my life I came to grips with just how heinous and evil sin is. For the first time in my life I saw my sin first and foremost as what I have done to God, to His Person. For the first time in my life I had godly sorrow that leads to true repentance and I had it only because God *granted* it to me. Now, God is far more beautiful and the Gospel far more precious to me than ever before. The Truth that I once knew and knew well intellectually has now killed me and created in me a new heart. That salvation is a gift and has nothing to do with human merit I have known intellectually for many years, but now I know it experientially. The doctrines of grace to which I had given a (begrudging) intellectual affirmation but still inwardly fought against are now glorious and precious to me because I have seen them played out in my life. God has saved me in spite of me. I now understand that He was under no obligation to do so, that I am wholly undeserving of this great gift and have absolutely nothing to contribute to it. God and God alone receives the glory for He and He alone deserves it.

Vince and Lori's Baptism together on July 31, 2011

At Fellowship Church with the Rev Run series promo sign

An example of seeker friendly worship with big screens, lights and lasers at Fellowship Church

Seeker Friendly VIP sign as you drive into Fellowship Church

At Grace Community Church in Sun Valley California, Pastor Dr John MacArthur

The sanctuary of Grace Community Church during a service, a holy and reverent moment.

At the offices of Living Waters in Bellflower California for a tour. Notice the sign above...we didn't pass the good person test.

With Phil Johnson at the Psalm 119 Conference in Fort Worth Texas. An amazing time of fellowship and growth through biblical preaching.

At the Deeper Conference in California with the team of Living waters, Mark Spence, Vince, Lori, and Ray Comfort

Tips on Tracting

Creative Ways to Spread the Gospel

Start off with visiting a website such as www.livingwaters.com to orders some tracts. They have a starter pack that has a sampling of tracts that you can see which ones work best for you. Once you have your tracts, figure out a way to keep them on you or with you at all times. That is key. If you are a female getting a purse that has lots of pouches and pockets on the outside helps give easy access to handing out a tract at check out lines or when out running errands.

Great Places to Leave Tracts:

- on the windshields of cars
- put them in with your bills when you are mailing them in
- tuck them into a book at a bookstore
- leave them on top of the free magazines outside of restaurants
- put it on top of the receipt after you pay at a restaurant for the waiter
- leave them on the table at the restaurant for the busboy

- make a baked good and attach it to the wrapping and give to a neighbor
- tuck it into a birthday or Christmas card
- leave it in the barrel at the bank where you normally put your deposit, just stick it inside when it comes back
- leave it on the handle at the pump of a gas station
- put them up on your bulletin board at your work desk or other obvious spot in your area

If you have not watched the documentary from Living Waters entitled 180, please do so. The resource link is on the Recommend Resources Page. They have t-shirts that promote the documentary. This is a powerful way to get not just the 180 documentary out, but also to promote the Gospel because it's presented in the documentary. Wear the t-shirts especially when traveling, you can actively witness just by what you are wearing. Vince and I wear them out together a lot of times because it gets a bigger reaction and notice from people. Be sure to have some 180 tracts on hand or the actual dvd which can be purchased on www.livingwaters.com

There are many creative ways to spread the Gospel, think outside of the box and pass out tracts, strike up conversations to change from the natural to the super natural. Most importantly, be equipped and read your Bible to know how to witness effectively the way Jesus did.

Recommended Resources Page

Grace to You, John Macarthur's Ministry—www.gty.org

Justin Peters Ministry on the Word of Faith movement—www.justinpeters.org

Phil Johnson's blogs— *www.teampyro.blogspot.com* and *www.spurgeon.org*

Living Waters, Ray Comfort's Ministry-www.livingwaters.com

The 180 movie direct link--www.180movie.com

Worldview Weekend with Brannon Howse—www.worldviewweekend.com

Grace Community Church's Book store—www.gbibooks.com

Ken Hamm's, Answers in Genesis—www.answersingenesis.org

Steve Green Ministries (music)—www.stevegreenministries.org

Sons of Korah (music)—www.sonsofkorah.com (or look them up on amazon)

Trisha Ramos's ministry—www.fishwithtrish.com

Art Azurdia's sermons—google his name and an archive list should come up

Joe Schimmel (pastor and exposes topics rightly) *www.goodfight.org*

Chris Pinto's ministry—www.noiseofthunder.com and *www.adullamfilms.com*

Caryl Matrisciana (exposes new age and other topics) *http://www.carylmatrisciana.com*

R.W Glenn (great expository preacher)—www.solidfoodmedia.com

Paul Washer's Ministry- www.heartcrymissionary.com

Links Showing Examples of Seeker Sensitive Churches

"Children's video – Dogs of Glory by Jim Steager - *http://www.youtube.com/watch?v=2oOHZvAYmxk&feature=player_embedded*

A Series from "Pastor" Ed Young Jr's Fellowship Church "Get Swaggerfied" - *http://www.youtube.com/watch?v=MpBn3joBvSk*

Ed Young Jr's U.B.U. Rap song "U.B.U." - *http://www.youtube.com/watch?v=LQcp-J-3njw&feature=relmfu*

Another attempt from "Pastor" Ed Young Jr. at rapping - a promo for a conference -
"HNL Hillsong 2010" -*http://www.youtube.com/watch?v=zGfpUsfz0kc&feature=relmfu*

"Pastor" Steven Furtick of Elevation Church giving his opinion of the purpose of the church – his church, at least
"What is the purpose of church?" - *http://www.youtube.com/watch?v=8wILPzCyWYk*

Steven Furtick's "Hey Haters" video
http://www.youtube.com/watch?v=NCW9-MglCsw&feature=related

"Sun Stand Still - Just Believe!" (Except from one of his visits to LifeChurch.tv) - http://www.youtube.com/watch?v=4wz9eMq8UMw&feature=fvsr

"Kumbaya - Elevation Church" - http://www.youtube.com/watch?feature=player_embedded&v=atkXB3j8zQo

"Discernment Guilt Trip? - Bereans Not Welcome" – Steven Furtick - http://www.youtube.com/watch?feature=player_embedded&v=DVqD4EWozII

"All Things New" - ELEVATION WORSHIP - http://www.youtube.com/watch?feature=player_embedded&v=Yb1h4nxyVtU
"I'm A Prodigy" Light Suit Element – Steven Furtick's Elevation church - http://vimeo.com/28854949
"Pastor" Perry Noble of NewSpring church
"March 20-2011 Perry Noble Says He Purposely Tries To Anger Religious People Sometimes" - http://www.youtube.com/watch?v=knLQu4QS660

"Seeker-Driven Prophet-Pastor Perry Noble Says Jack--- In Church Wants Deeper Teaching" - http://www.youtube.com/watch?v=rQEC1bZN3BU&feature=related

"Seeker Driven Prophet-Pastor Perry Noble Tells Church He Doesn't Want To Know Them" - http://www.youtube.com/watch?v=zOBZldF6Y0M&feature=related

"Perry Noble Tells Church Members: "You Officially *** as a Human Being" If You Don't Like the Music" - http://vimeo.com/26050869

"North Point Church does Hero by Foo Fighters for Easter 2010" - http://www.youtube.com/watch?v=g4D6ZxH1r0Q

"North Point Church does Thriller" - http://www.youtube.com/watch?v=kX1Sjajl550&feature=related

"Hell's Bells" at Northpoint Church - http://www.youtube.com/watch?v=ixO-GehIUgM&feature=related

"Sympathy For The Devil" – Northpoint church, Missouri - http://www.youtube.com/watch?feature=player_embedded&v=Dz7hYUjoPzQ

"WHY behind Spa City Stomp Out" – Lakepoint church - http://www.youtube.com/watch?feature=player_embedded&v=51MhplShvEM#!

"Crosspoint: At the Movies" - http://vimeo.com/24117706

"Boom Boom Pow" - ("Christian" Version) - http://www.youtube.com/watch?feature=player_embedded&v=jue3KPrDQiA

"Whoopee Cushion Life Teaser" – Northpoint church series - http://vimeo.com/18429898

"Bringing Serving Back" – Parkview Christian church - http://vimeo.com/16596080

"Saddle Up And Ride" – Family Christian Center - http://vimeo.com/10965208

"B-SHOC - JESUS LEAN Music Video" - http://www.youtube.com/watch?v=8D7iT2MT00o&feature=player_embedded

"Does your youth pastor get krunk? . . . ours does." - http://www.youtube.com/watch?v=TBtPtytOZCo&feature=player_embedded

Life Groups Music Video - "Thug Life" - *http://vimeo.com/14930410*

Pastor Steve Invite: Two52 JUDAH SMITH - *http://vimeo.com/13658598*

"Official GCC Plays Simon" – Granger Community Church *http://vimeo.com/14029417*

"Church by the Glades - *Van Halen* "Jump!" - *http://www.youtube.com/watch?v=6K0O01JiBoc&feature=player_embedded*

"The Adventures of the StoneBridge Staff Episode 1" - *http://www.youtube.com/watch?v=tfYlSJ_IllE&feature=player_embedded*

"MOJO's in the Air" - Heartland Christian Center" - *http://www.youtube.com/watch?v=Hr8uloVxlEw&feature=player_embedded*

"4th of July Rodeo Commercial" – Cornerstone Church - *http://vimeo.com/12110364*

"Fellowship Church - Tithe Rap" - *http://www.youtube.com/watch?v=jbv9UBgvGz4&feature=player_embedded*

"JESUS IS BETTER THAN FOOTBALL" - *http://www.youtube.com/watch?v=zDj3WZUXCmw&feature=player_embedded*

Church Announcements, Seeker-Driven Style - North Point News Rap (10-17/18-09) - *http://www.youtube.com/watch?v=PXUo_8vP_Zo&feature=player_embedded*

"Rick Warren on a life of purpose" - *http://www.ted.com/talks/rick_warren_on_a_life_of_purpose.html*

"Highlights from the Global Leadership Summit 2011" – (Annual Leadership Conference hosted by Bill Hybels) *http://www.youtube.com/watch?v=ydc29l-1M6Q&feature=topics*

"More On Bill Hybels" - *http://www.youtube.com/watch?v=crx2cZO0MbU&feature=topics*

"Joel Osteen Doesn't Know" - *http://www.youtube.com/watch?v=kx_El_yA-eI&feature=related*

"Joel Osteen Says Jesus Christ is Not the Only Way" - *http://www.youtube.com/watch?v=KwL1DThtxYg&feature=related*

Links to Great Preachers Boldly Preaching the Word

"The Truth: Lawson's Rebuke of Osteen" - *http://www.youtube.com/watch?v=D7n2BObju9M&feature=related*

"John MacArthur Rebukes Joel Osteen" - *http://www.youtube.com/watch?v=jDuDN2FtrIo&feature=related*

"Rev. Franklin Graham: Rob Bell Is A "False Teacher" & A "Heretic" - *http://www.youtube.com/watch?v=fCOkGDUgij8&feature=related*

Dr John MacArthur talks about Rick Warren's best-selling book – "MacArthur on the Purpose Driven Life" *http://www.youtube.com/watch?v=nI9EzMWZoag&feature=related*

Dr John MacArthur – "Never Make a Gospel Appeal to People's Emotions" - *http://www.youtube.com/watch?v=y5ZRb2BByUg&feature=related*

Dr. Steve Lawson – "It Will Cost You Everything" - *http://www.youtube.com/watch?v=5JQOBMi4QS8*

"Paul Washer's Testimony - Let me tell about my Jesus" - *http://www.youtube.com/watch?v=LyXDYb5Z0cY*

"Come to Christ, He is Mighty to Save - Paul Washer" - *http://www.youtube.com/watch?v=ZbWaIvB_heo&feature=player_embedded*

"Do You Desire God? - Paul Washer" - *http://www.youtube.com/watch?v=ngSq7mABZGE&feature=relmfu*

"The Power of the Holy Spirit is Essential" – Paul Washer – *http://illbehonest.com/The-Power-of-the-Holy-Spirit-is-Essential-Paul-Washer*

"Powerful Testimonies From Former False Converts" *http://www.youtube.com/watch?v=Tcqu2WjSOJo&feature=related*

"The Prayer that Damns Many to Hell" – James Jennings – www.illbehonest.com
http://www.youtube.com/watch?v=DXYu6x9ywLU&feature=related

Bibliography

1. Way of the Master, A Living Waters production. <www.livingwaters.com.>

2. Silva, Ken. "Fuller Theological Seminary Birthed Church Growth Movement." 10 July 2010 <http://apprising.org/2010/07/10/fuller-theological-seminary-birthed-church-growth-movement/>.

3. Brachear, Manya A. "Rev Bill Hybels: the father of Willow Creek." Chicago Tribune. Chicago Tribune News. Web. 6 August 2006.

4. Smith, Warren. Deceived on Purpose. Magalia, CA.: Mountain Stream Press, 2004.

5. Oppenheimer, Mike. "The Seeker Friendly Church Model." 2011<http://www.letusreason.org/Popteac25.html>.

6. Silva, Ken. "John MacArthur: Seeker-Friendly Movement is the New Liberalism." 7 May 2009 < http://apprising.org/2009/05/07/john-macarthur-

seeker-friendly-movement-is-the-new-liberalism/>.

7. Fox, Marisa (4 July 1990). "Pop a la Mode"-. Spin 6 (4). Retrieved 10 August 2011.

8. John Macarthur Study Bible NASB study notes 2 Timothy 3:16.

9. Dever, Mark. "9 Marks Explained, Q and A for Pastors." 2011<http://www.9marks.org/answers/according-scripture-why-should-every-christian-join-church>.

10. Way of the Master, The Good Person Test. Living Waters Ministry, Ray Comfort.

11. Comfort, Ray. The Way of the Master. Alachua, Florida.: Bridge-Logos, 2006.

12. Refer to interview by Martin Bashir of Rob Bell on March 15, 2011, MSNBC News.

13. Azurdia, Art. "God Saves Bad People." 2009<http://www.youtube.com/watch?v=hoMIDK1SXTU>.

14. Macarthur, John. Wwwgty.org, Sermons Entitled 4 Marks of the Man of God and The Man of God.

15. Green, Don. Grace Community Church sermon "How to Recognize True Repentance".

16. Testimony of David Berkowitz, < http://www.ariseandshine.org/Testimony-&-Translations.html>.

Made in the USA
Lexington, KY
06 April 2012